Contents

KT-376-681

Acknowledgements

The author and publishers are grateful to those authors, publishers and others who have given permission for the use of copyright material identified in the text. It has not always been possible to identify the source of material used or to contact the copyright holders and in such cases the publishers would welcome information from the copyright owners.

The Co-operative Group for text on p. 19: Co-operative Young Film-makers of the Year. © The Co-operative Group. Co-operative Young Film Makers Festival; *Brighton & Hove Leader* for adapted text on p. 20: 'Leisure Centre Plans' by Cliff Taylor. 11 September 1998. © Newsquest Media Group; *Cambridge Evening News* for adapted text on pp. 42–43: 'Singing means living in perfect harmony. © Cambridge Newspapers 2006; Rachel Spence for adapted text on p. 64: 'How would you handle being rich?', *The Guardian*, 3 June 2000. Used by kind permission of Rachel Spence; *The Young Telegraph* for adapted text on p. 67: 'On top of the World', April 1998. © Telegraph Group Limited, 1998; Michael Eboda for adapted text on p. 86: 'Breaking the Ice', *The Sunday Times*, 9 November 1997. Used by kind permission of Michael Eboda; Jacqui Swift for adapted text on p. 88: 'Webcareers.com', *Daily Telegraph*, 19 February 2000. Used by kind permission of Jacqui Swift.

For permission to reproduce photographs:

Alamy for pp. 22, 25, 30, 47, 74, 96, 107 (5) (Photofusion Picture Library); Corbis for pp. 44, 52, 66, 96, 103 (2); Getty Images for pp. 105, 109 (7 & 9); www.johnbirdsall.co.uk for p. 103 (1); Superstock for p. 107 (6); TIPS Images for p. 109 (8).

Picture research by Kevin Brown

Cover design by OptaDesign

The audio CDs which accompany this book were recorded at Studio AVP, London.

CAMBRIDGE

Exams Extra

PET

WITH ANSWERS

CAMBRIDGE UNIVERSITY PRESS
Cambridge, New York, Melbourne, Madrid, Cape Town, Singapore, São Paulo

Cambridge University Press
The Edinburgh Building, Cambridge CB2 2RU, UK

www.cambridge.org
Information on this title: www.cambridge.org/9780521676687

First published 2006

Printed in the United Kingdom at the University Press, Cambridge

A catalogue record for this book is available from the British Library

ISBN-13 978 0 521 676687 Student's Book with answers and CD-ROM
ISBN-10 0 521 676681 Student's Book with answers and CD-ROM

ISBN-13 978 0 521 676670 Student's Book
ISBN-10 0 521 676673 Student's Book

ISBN-13 978 0 521 676694 Audio CD Set
ISBN-10 0 521 67669X Audio CD Set

ISBN-13 978 0 521 676700 Self-study Pack
ISBN-10 0 521 676703 Self-study Pack

INTRODUCTION

Who is this book for?

Cambridge Exams Extra – PET is for anyone preparing to take the Cambridge ESOL Preliminary English Test (PET). It can be used at home or in class with a teacher.

What is in this book?

Cambridge Exams Extra – PET includes four PET past papers from Cambridge ESOL. Each of the four tests includes a Reading and Writing Test, a Listening Test and a Speaking Test. Before each part of each test there are tips and exercises to help students prepare fully. There are also detailed notes giving information about PET, including what each paper consists of and how the exam is marked (see 'A guide to PET' on page 6). The book is accompanied by a set of two audio CDs.

Cambridge Exams Extra – PET is available in two editions: one with answers and one without. The 'with answers' edition contains answers to all questions, including authentic sample answers for the Writing Test, as well as complete recording scripts of the audio CDs. It also includes a CD-ROM containing the same four Reading, Writing and Listening tests that appear in the book, enabling students to practise for the computer-based PET. Both editions also contain specimen answer sheets which can be photocopied and used for practice.

How can I use this book?

Cambridge Exams Extra – PET is organised by test paper. You can use the book in any order you wish. For example, if you would like to practise for the Listening Test, you can go directly to this section in each test.

The extra exercises before each part of each test should be done before the actual tests are attempted. These exercises highlight the problem areas of each test and give suggestions for how to deal with them.

In the Reading and Writing Test, sample answers to the writing are supplied with examiner's band scores in the 'with answers' edition. Tips will advise you on how to improve your writing skills, telling you what you should and shouldn't do. You can then compare your own answer to the sample answers.

You should always do the Listening Test without looking at the script. However, after you have finished the test, you can use the script to confirm what you have understood.

The Speaking Test is better practised with a partner. However, the book gives you exercises to practise by yourself and tips to help you think about how to improve.

The PET examination is part of a group of examinations developed by Cambridge ESOL called the Cambridge Main Suite. The Main Suite consists of five examinations which have similar characteristics but are designed for different levels of English language ability. Within the five levels, PET is at level B1 (Threshold) in the *Council of Europe's Common European Framework of Reference for Languages: Learning, teaching, assessment*. It has also been accredited by the Qualifications and Curriculum Authority in the UK as an Entry Level 3 ESOL certificate in the National Qualifications Framework.

Examination	Council of Europe Framework Level	UK National Qualifications Framework Level
CPE Certificate of Proficiency in English	C2	3
CAE Certificate in Advanced English	C1	2
FCE First Certificate in English	B2	1
PET Preliminary English Test	B1	Entry 3
KET Key English Test	A2	Entry 2

PET is taken by more than 80,000 people each year in more than 80 countries, and is a valuable qualification if you want to work or study abroad or to develop a career in international business. It is also useful preparation for higher level exams, such as FCE (First Certificate in English), CAE (Certificate in Advanced English) and CPE (Certificate of Proficiency in English).

If you can deal with everyday written and spoken communications (e.g. read simple textbooks and articles, write simple personal letters, make notes during a meeting), then this is the exam for you.

Topics

These are the topics used in the PET exam:

Clothes	Hobbies and leisure	Transport
Daily life	House and home	Services
Education	Language	Shopping
Entertainment and media	People	Social interaction
Environment	Personal feelings, opinions and experiences	Sport
Food and drink		The natural world
Free time	Personal identification	Travel and holidays
Health, medicine and exercise	Places and buildings	Weather
	Relations with other people	Work and jobs

PET content: an overview

Paper	Name	Timing	Content	Test focus
Paper 1	Reading/ Writing	1 hour 30 minutes	Reading: Five parts which test a range of reading skills with a variety of texts, ranging from very short notices to longer continuous texts. Writing: Three parts which test a range of writing skills.	Assessment of candidates' ability to understand the meaning of written English at word, phrase, sentence, paragraph and whole text level. Assessment of candidates' ability to produce straightforward written English, ranging from producing variations on simple sentences to pieces of continuous text.
Paper 2	Listening	30 minutes (approx.)	Four parts ranging from short exchanges to longer dialogues and monologues.	Assessment of candidates' ability to understand dialogues and monologues in both informal and neutral settings on a range of everyday topics.
Paper 3	Speaking	10–12 minutes per pair of candidates	Four parts: In Part 1, candidates interact with an examiner; In Parts 2 and 4 they interact with another candidate; In Part 3, they have an extended individual long turn.	Assessment of candidates' ability to express themselves in order to carry out functions at *Threshold* level. To ask and to understand questions and make appropriate responses. To talk freely on matters of personal interest.

Paper 1: Reading and Writing

Paper format
The Reading component contains five parts. The Writing component contains three parts.

Number of questions
Reading has 35 questions; Writing has seven questions.

Sources
Authentic and adapted-authentic real world notices; newspapers and magazines; simplified encyclopaedias; brochures and leaflets; websites.

Answering
Candidates indicate answers by shading lozenges (Reading), or writing answers (Writing) on an answer sheet.

Timing
1 hour 30 minutes.

Marks
Reading: Each of the 35 questions carries one mark. This is weighted so that this comprises 25% of total marks for the whole examination.
Writing: Questions 1–5 carry one mark each. Question 6 is marked out of five; and question 7/8 is marked out of 15. This gives a total of 25 which represents 25% of total marks for the whole examination.

Preparing for the Reading component

To prepare for the Reading component, you should read a variety of authentic texts, for example, newspapers and magazines, non-fiction books, and other sources of factual material, such as leaflets, brochures and websites. It is also a good idea to practise reading (and writing) short communicative messages, including notes, cards and emails. Remember you won't always need to understand every word in order to be able to do a task in the exam.

Before the examination, think about the time you need to do each part. It is usually approximately 50 minutes on the Reading component and 40 minutes on the Writing component.

Reading			
Part	Task Type and Format	Task Focus	Number of questions
1	Three-option multiple choice. Five very short discrete texts; signs and messages, postcards, notes, emails, labels etc., plus one example.	Reading real-world notices and other short texts for the main message.	5
2	Matching. Five items in the form of descriptions of people to match to eight short adapted-authentic texts.	Reading multiple texts for specific information and detailed comprehension.	5
3	True/False. Ten items with an adapted-authentic long text.	Processing a factual text. Scanning for specific information while disregarding redundant material.	10
4	Four-option multiple choice. Five items with an adapted-authentic long text.	Reading for detailed comprehension; understanding attitude, opinion and writer purpose. Reading for gist, inference and global meaning.	5
5	Four-option multiple-choice cloze. Ten items, plus an integrated example, with an adapted-authentic text drawn from a variety of sources. The text is of a factual or narrative nature.	Understanding of vocabulary and grammar in a short text, and understanding the lexico-structural patterns in the text.	10

Preparing for the Writing component

Part 1

You have to complete five sentences which will test your grammar. There is an example, showing exactly what the task involves. You should write between one and three words to fill this gap. The second sentence, when complete, must mean the same as the first sentence.

It is essential to spell correctly and no marks will be given if a word is misspelled. You will also lose the mark if you produce an answer of more than three words, even if your writing includes the correct answer.

Part 2

You have to produce a short communicative message of between 35 and 45 words in length. You are told who you are writing to and why, and you must include three content points. These are clearly laid out with bullet points in the question. To gain top marks, all three points must be in your answer, so it is important to read the question carefully and plan what you will include. Marks will not be deducted for small errors.

Before the exam, you need to practise writing answers of the correct length. Answers that are too short or too long will probably lose marks.

The General Mark Scheme below is used with a Task-specific Mark Scheme (see pages 111, 117, 124 and 130).

General Mark Scheme for Writing Part 2

Mark	Criteria
5	All content elements covered appropriately. Message clearly communicated to reader.
4	All content elements adequately dealt with. Message communicated successfully, on the whole.
3	All content elements attempted. Message requires some effort by the reader. or One content element omitted but others clearly communicated.
2	Two content elements omitted, or unsuccessfully dealt with. Message only partly communicated to reader. or Script may be slightly short (20–25 words).
1	Little relevant content and/or message requires excessive effort by the reader, or short (10–19 words).
0	Totally irrelevant or totally incomprehensible or too short (under 10 words).

Part 3

You have a choice of task: either a story or an informal letter. You need to write about 100 words for both tasks. Answers below 80 words will receive fewer marks. Answers longer than 100 words may receive fewer marks.

Make sure you practise enough before the exam. Reading simplified readers in English will give you ideas for story writing. Also writing to a penfriend or e-pal will give you useful practice.

Mark Scheme for Writing Part 3

Band 5 – the candidate's writing fully achieves the desired effect on the target reader. The use of language will be confident and ambitious for the level, including a wide range of structures and vocabulary within the task set. Coherence, within the constraints of the level, will be achieved by the use of simple linking devices, and the response will be well organised. Errors which do occur will be minor and non-impeding, perhaps due to ambitious attempts at more complex language. Overall, no effort will be required of the reader.

Band 4 – the candidate's writing will achieve the desired effect on the target reader. The use of language will be fairly ambitious for the level, including a range of structures and vocabulary within the task set. There will be some linking of sentences and evidence of organisation. Some errors will occur, although these will be generally non-impeding. Overall, only a little effort will be required of the reader.

Band 3 – the candidate's writing may struggle at times to achieve the desired effect on the target reader. The use of language, including the range of structure and vocabulary, will be unambitious, or, if ambitious, it will be flawed. There will be some attempt at organisation but the linking of sentences will not always be maintained. A number of errors may be present, although these will be mostly non-impeding. Overall, some effort will be required of the reader.

Band 2 – the candidate's writing struggles to achieve the desired effect on the target reader. The use of language, including the range of structure and vocabulary, will tend to be simplistic, limited, or repetitive. The response may be incoherent, and include erratic use of punctuation. There will be numerous errors which will sometimes impede communication. Overall, considerable effort will be required of the reader.

Band 1 – the candidate's writing has a negative effect on the target reader. The use of language will be severely restricted, and there will be no evidence of a range of structures and vocabulary. The response will be seriously incoherent, and may include an absence of punctuation. Language will be very poorly controlled and the response will be difficult to understand. Overall, excessive effort will be required of the reader.

Band 0 – there may be too little language for assessment, or the response may be totally illegible; the content may be impossible to understand, or completely irrelevant to the task.

Writing			
Part	**Task Type and Format**	**Task Focus**	**Number of questions**
1	Sentence transformations. Five items, plus an integrated example, that are theme-related. Candidates are given sentences and then asked to complete similar sentences using a different structural pattern so that the sentence still has the same meaning.	Control and understanding of Threshold/PET grammatical structures. Rephrasing and reformulating information.	5
2	Short communicative message. Candidates are prompted to write a short message in the form of a postcard, note, email, etc. The prompt takes the form of a rubric to respond to.	A short piece of writing of 35–45 words focusing on communication of specific messages.	1
3	A longer piece of continuous writing. There is a choice of two questions, an informal letter or a story. Candidates are primarily assessed on their ability to use and control a range of Threshold-level language. Coherent organisation, spelling and punctuation are also assessed.	Writing about 100 words focusing on control and range of language.	1

Paper 2: Listening

Paper format
This paper contains four parts.

Number of questions
25

Text types
All texts are based on authentic situations.

Answering
Candidates indicate answers either by shading lozenges (Parts 1, 2 and 4) or writing answers (Part 3) on an answer sheet. Candidates record their answers on the question paper as they listen. They are then given six minutes at the end of the test to copy these on to the answer sheet.

Recording information
Each text is heard twice. Recordings will contain a variety of accents corresponding to standard variants of native speaker accents.

Timing
About 30 minutes, plus six minutes to transfer answers.

Marking
Each item carries one mark. This gives a total of 25 marks, which represents 25% of total marks for the whole examination.

Part	Task Type and Format	Task Focus	Number of questions
1	Multiple choice (discrete). Short neutral or informal monologues or dialogues. Seven discrete three-option multiple-choice items with visuals, plus one example.	Listening to identify key information from short exchanges.	7
2	Multiple choice. Longer monologue or interview (with one main speaker). Six three-option multiple-choice items.	Listening to identify specific information and detailed meaning.	6
3	Gap-fill. Longer monologue. Six gaps to fill in. Candidates need to write one or more words in each space.	Listening to identify, understand and interpret information.	6
4	True/False. Longer informal dialogue. Candidates need to decide whether six statements are correct or incorrect.	Listening for detailed meaning, and to identify the attitudes and opinions of the speakers.	6

Preparing for the Listening paper

You will hear the instructions for each task on the tape, and see them on the exam paper. In Part 1, there is also an example text and task to show you how to record your answers. In Parts 2, 3 and 4, the instructions are followed by a pause; you should read the questions in that part then. This will help you prepare for the listening.

The best preparation for the listening paper is to listen to authentic spoken English at this level. Having discussions provides a good authentic source of listening practice, as does listening to the teacher. You can also listen to texts on tape to give you practice in understanding different voices and styles of delivery.

Paper 3: Speaking

Paper format
The standard format is two candidates and two examiners. One of the examiners acts as an interlocutor and the other as an assessor. The interlocutor directs the test, while the assessor takes no part in the interaction.

Timing
10–12 minutes per pair of candidates.

Marks
Candidates are assessed on their performance throughout the test. There are a total of 25 marks in Paper 3, making 25% of the total score for the whole examination.

Part	Task Type and Format	Task Focus	Timing
1	Each candidate interacts with the interlocutor. The interlocutor asks the candidates questions in turn, using standardised questions.	Giving information of a factual, personal kind. The candidates respond to questions about present circumstances, past experiences and future plans.	2–3 minutes
2	Simulated situation. Candidates interact with each other. Visual stimulus is given to the candidates to aid the discussion task. The interlocutor sets up the activity using a standardised rubric.	Using functional language to make and respond to suggestions, discuss alternatives, make recommendations and negotiate agreement.	2–3 minutes
3	Extended turn. A colour photograph is given to each candidate in turn and they are asked to talk about it for up to a minute. Both photographs relate to the same topic.	Describing photographs and managing discourse, using appropriate vocabulary, in a longer turn.	3 minutes
4	General conversation. Candidates interact with each other. The topic of the conversation develops the theme established in Part 3. The interlocutor sets up the activity using a standardised rubric.	The candidates talk together about their opinions, likes/dislikes, preferences, experiences, habits etc.	3 minutes

Assessment

Throughout the test, you are assessed on your language skills, not your personality, intelligence or knowledge of the world. You must, however, be prepared to develop the conversation, where appropriate, and respond to the tasks set. Prepared speeches are not acceptable.

You are assessed on your own individual performance and not in relation to each other. Both examiners assess you. The interlocutor awards a mark for global achievement; the assessor awards marks according to: Grammar and Vocabulary, Discourse Management, Pronunciation and Interactive Communication.

Grammar and Vocabulary
This refers to the accurate and appropriate use of grammatical forms and vocabulary. It also includes the range of both grammatical forms and vocabulary. Performance is viewed in terms of the overall effectiveness of the language used in dealing with the tasks.

Discourse Management
This refers to the coherence, extent and relevance of each individual's contribution. On this scale, the ability to maintain a coherent flow of language is assessed, either within a single utterance or over a string of utterances. Also assessed here is how relevant the contributions are to what has gone before.

Pronunciation
This refers to the candidate's ability to produce comprehensible utterances to fulfil the task requirements. This includes stress, rhythm and intonation, as well as individual sounds. Examiners put themselves in the position of the non-language specialist and assess the overall impact of the pronunciation and the degree of effort required to understand the candidate. Different varieties of English e.g. British, North American, Australian etc., are acceptable, provided they are used consistently throughout the test.

Interactive Communication
This scale refers to the candidate's ability to use language to achieve meaningful communication. This includes initiating and responding without undue hesitation, the ability to use interactive strategies to maintain or repair communication, and sensitivity to the norms of turn-taking.

Further information

The information contained in this practice book is designed to be an overview of the exam. For a full description of all of the above exams including information about task types, testing focus and preparation, please see the relevant handbooks which can be obtained from Cambridge ESOL at the address below or from the website at www.CambridgeESOL.org

University of Cambridge ESOL Examinations
1 Hills Road
Cambridge CB1 2EU
United Kingdom

Telephone +44 1223 553355
Fax: +44 1223 460278
e-mail: ESOLHelpdesk@Cambridgeassessment.org.uk

TEST 1

Reading ● PART 1

TIP

Read the notices and messages first. Don't look at the A/B/C choices until you understand the texts.

Look at each notice or message opposite. Don't read the A/B/C choices yet.

Question 1

1 Where would you probably see this notice?
   A at the entrance to the bookshop café
   B at the cash desk in the bookshop

2 Must you buy the books
   A before you go into the café?
   B when you're in the café?

3 Complete this statement:
   If you haven't already bought the books, you can't .... into the café.

Now look at the A/B/C choices and circle your answer.

Question 2

1 How long can you use the equipment?
   A no more than 15 minutes
   B minimum of 15 minutes

2 Does this time limit apply
   A always?
   B sometimes?

3 Complete this statement:
   You can't use this equipment for .... 15 minutes at certain times.

Now look at the A/B/C choices and circle your answer.

Question 3

1 What's the reason for this notice?
   A to tell people about a new bus service
   B to tell people about the times for this bus service

2 Does the 22 bus service operate
   A all day?   B for a few hours a day?

3 Complete this statement:
   The 22 bus service will not operate along Regent Street .... 10 a.m.

Now look at the A/B/C choices and circle your answer.

Question 4

1 Who do you think put this notice on the board?
   A students at the college
   B the administration of the college

2 Which action should you do first?
   A leave the room
   B turn off the fans

3 Why is it important to turn off the fans?
   A to save money
   B to stop accidents

Now look at the A/B/C choices and circle your answer.

Question 5

1 Where would you see this notice?
   A on the parcel   B inside the parcel

2 Does the parcel have a handle?
   A yes   B no

3 Complete this statement:
   There are things inside this parcel that might .... if you're not ....

Now look at the A/B/C choices and circle your answer.

Part 1

Questions 1–5

Look at the text in each question.
What does it say?
Mark the correct letter A, B, or C on your answer sheet.

Example:

0

REGENCY CAMERAS

Buy two films
and get one
FREE

A   Buy three films for the price of two.

B   Get a free film with every one you buy.

C   One film free with each camera.

Answer:

0	A	B	C
	▬	▭	▭

1

ONLY BOOKS ALREADY PAID FOR CAN BE TAKEN INTO THE BOOKSHOP CAFÉ

A   Do not read our books while you are eating in the café.

B   Pay in the café for any books that you want to buy.

C   Do not take books which you haven't bought yet into the café.

2

CENTRAL GYM

15-minute limit on the use of equipment at busy times

A   Equipment is available for a maximum of 15 minutes at any time.

B   When the gym is crowded, there is a time limit for using the equipment.

C   At busy times you may have to queue to use the equipment.

3

From 3 January the 22 bus service will operate along Regent Street 7–10 a.m. only

A   A new 22 bus will operate along Regent Street from 3 January.

B   After 3 January you can catch a 22 bus all day on Regent Street.

C   There will be a limited 22 bus service along Regent Street from 3 January.

4

BARTON COLLEGE

TO REDUCE ELECTRICITY COSTS, PLEASE TURN OFF ALL FANS BEFORE LEAVING ROOMS

A   Save us money by switching off fans when you finish using a room.

B   When you leave, please replace any fans you have borrowed from other rooms.

C   Please lock away all fans before leaving the room.

5

Handle with care – breakable goods inside parcel

A   Be careful with this parcel as the goods might break.

B   Use the handle to pick up this parcel so the goods won't break.

C   Take care when wrapping parcels with breakable goods inside.

TIP

It's important to work out what the different people want before you look at the eight texts.

What do the people want?

First, read the instructions below. Then, look at the people (6–10) and underline what they want.

There are four pieces of important information to underline in questions 6, 9 and 10, and three pieces in questions 7 and 8. The first question has been done for you as an example.

Look at the texts about the beaches. There are three extra texts that have no match. These are texts B, E, G. Cross them out.

Now read the other texts and answer these questions.

Read text A   Hadwick

1   Why is this beach not suitable for people in questions 6 and 10?

2   Why is this beach not suitable for people in question 7?

3   So which people (question 8 or 9) does it match?

Read text C   Amrith

4   There is something missing from this beach which makes it unsuitable for people in question 6. What is it?

5   Why is this beach not suitable for people in question 7?

6   So which people (question 8 or 10) does it match?

Read text D   Torsands

7   What two reasons make this beach unsuitable for people in question 6?

8   Is it a better match for people in question 7 or 8?

Read text F   Halcombe

9   What two reasons make this beach unsuitable for the people in question 6?

10 Does it match all the requirements of people in question 8? Check all three things that you underlined.

Read text H   Marple

11 Check that this beach is a good match for the final group of people.

Part 2

Questions 6–10

The people below all want to spend a day by the sea.
On the opposite page there are descriptions of eight beaches.
Decide which beach would be the most suitable for the following people.
For questions **6–10** mark the correct letter **(A–H)** on your answer sheet.

6    Philip and Jenny have two children who cannot swim. Jenny wants them to be able to play safely in the water. Philip wants to learn to sail. They need to park near the beach.

7    Marco and Sandra want to spend the day on the beach and have lunch in a café. Marco wants to go surfing, while Sandra wants to relax in the sun.

8 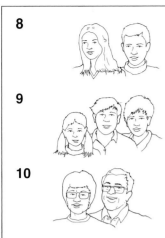 Remi and Claudia want to relax on the beach. Remi would also like to do some sport, while Claudia would like to buy some presents to take home.

9 Richard, Fiona and their seven-year-old daughter want to swim and go for a walk. They would also like somewhere that has a children's play area, and they plan to buy souvenirs.

10 Paul and Rachel want somewhere with lots of space where they can sit and enjoy the view. Rachel would not manage a difficult walk to the beach. They want to eat lunch in a café.

BEACHES

A Hadwick

A sandy beach with lots of space and views out to Fishport Harbour. Surfing is not permitted but swimming is safe and there is a children's play area and a small shop. The nearest car park is two kilometres away. There are many pleasant walks along the coastal path.

B Godstow

A narrow beach which is surrounded by high cliffs and is popular for sunbathing, surfing and sailing. It is safe to swim here. It is next to Winburn Golf Club but there is no car park and the only access is along the coastal path. No café or shopping facilities.

C Amrith

A large beach which attracts quite a few visitors but doesn't get crowded because of its size. There are pleasant views out to sea and to Bedruth Island. Swimming is safe but surfing is not permitted. There is a café and parking but no shops.

D Torsands

A very sheltered beach which is great for sunbathing. It is a popular surfing and sailing beach but swimming is dangerous. There is a café and a children's play area but there is no car park and visitors have a ten-minute walk across fields.

E Portsea

The excellent views make this beach well worth a visit. There are shallow pools which are safe for children to play in. However, there are no roads to the beach and the only access is across fields, though this doesn't stop some keen surfers. There are no facilities here.

F Halcombe

This is a small beach within easy reach of the town centre and its many shops. It is very popular so there isn't much space. It is next to the Milgrove Golf Club, which is open to the public and has a restaurant. There is no children's play area, and surfing is not permitted.

G Fishport

A small beach which never gets crowded because there are many steep steps down to the beach and there is no car park. There is a small shop but no children's play area or café. Swimming is good and there are pleasant walks along the coastal path.

H Marple

Although unsuitable for surfing, this is a popular boating centre. Swimming is good and the many pools of shallow water are safe for children. Ocean Watersports Centre, which offers lessons in sailing and water skiing, is next to the beach. There is a steep path to the beach from the car park.

TIP

Read the sentences (questions 11–20) before you read the text.

First, read sentences 11–20 about a film-making competition.

Some words have been <u>underlined</u>. This is the information that you will need to look for when you read the text.

Remember, the underlined words in sentences 11–20 will probably not appear in the text – the text will use different words to say the same thing.

Questions 11, 14, 18, 20 are incorrect statements. Questions 12, 13, 15, 16, 17, 19 are correct statements.

Work through the text to decide why each sentence is correct or incorrect. For a sentence to be correct, you need to find a 'match' between the underlined words in the sentence and the words in the text.

Read quickly (scan) the first two paragraphs of the text and underline the parts that give you the answer to question 11:

Every year, Co-operative …
For over 30 years, the Co-operative …

Continue in the same way with questions 12–20.

Part 3

Questions 11–20

Look at the sentences below about a film-making competition.
Read the text on the opposite page to decide if each sentence is correct or incorrect.
If it is correct, mark **A** on your answer sheet.
If it is not correct, mark **B** on your answer sheet.

---

11   This is the first Co-operative film-making competition <u>for 30 years</u>.

12   You can enter the competition <u>without any experience of film-making</u>.

13   The Co-operative prefers <u>short films</u>.

14   The Co-operative will <u>lend you whatever you require to make your film</u>.

15   The Co-operative suggests putting <u>music in your film</u>.

16   The judges will watch <u>the whole of every film</u> entered.

17   If you <u>are 18</u> and enter the competition <u>this year</u>, you can <u>still enter it next year</u>.

18   Films entered in the competition are <u>all</u> screened at the festival.

19   The Co-operative pays for <u>some people</u> to attend the festival.

20   <u>Information packs</u> will be available from <u>11 May</u>.

Co-operative Young Film-makers of the Year

Have you got something to say? An idea for a great movie? An interesting documentary? Or an amusing comedy? Don't keep it to yourself. Get together with some friends, share your thoughts and make a film or video.

Every year, Co-operative Young Film-makers offers you the chance to see your work on the big screen. For over 30 years the Co-operative has organised a festival for young film-makers, proving how committed we are to young people and their films. We'll be holding this year's festival on Friday 9 and Saturday 10 October at the National Film Theatre.

We're looking for young film-makers with imagination. Whether you're already planning a career in the movies or have never made a film in your life, it doesn't matter. We want to see films and videos from people of all abilities and levels of experience.

NOW FOR OUR RULES AND SUGGESTIONS

 * You might be at school or college. Perhaps a member of a youth club or drama group. Maybe just a group of friends. The only thing we do say is that you have to be less than 21 years old in order to enter our competition.

 * We want to show as many films as we can on the big screen – the briefer the films, the more we can show. You can say a lot in the six minutes or less that we suggest. Especially if you plan your film in advance and edit it well.

 * You need to supply your own equipment – try borrowing from family and friends. Most types of film and video are acceptable. Just concentrate on getting the most out of your equipment. Experiment a bit!

 * Think of an interesting storyline. It'll help to make your work a bit different. We're really keen to get films about the environment or international issues. Why not try writing your own music?

Every film and video we receive is looked at by our group of judges. They watch each one from start to finish, then tell you what they think. This can really help if you are thinking about trying again in twelve months' time.

If your film is chosen for screening at the festival – and last year 50 were – you will get free entry to the festival, and we will cover any costs, such as your travel. The festival ends with a presentation on stage after your work is screened.

Get in touch before you start filming and we'll post you a full information pack. This will include a form to enter the competition and other details you need to consider.

Don't forget the competition closing date is Monday 11 May.

TIP

Some of the questions ask about facts and some ask about opinions. You'll always be able to find the answers in the text.

Read the text below once. It should take you about three minutes. After the first reading, you should have a general idea of what the text is about. Now answer these questions.

1 What do Cityspace want to build?

2 What's in that space at the moment?

3 Who is against the development?

4 What will the town lose if the development goes ahead?

5 What other disadvantages are mentioned about the development?

6 Does anyone in the town want the new development?

7 Who do you think the writer of this article is?

8 Do we learn anything about the writer's *own* opinion of the development?

Read the text again. It is very important to get a good understanding.

Read the questions below and see if you can write your own answers. Don't look at the A/B/C/D choices.

Question 21: What is the writer trying to do in the article?

Question 22: What will the reader discover from the article?

Question 23: What does the action group think about the new leisure centre?

Question 24: Which group of people is keen on having the new leisure centre?

Question 25: What would be a good headline for the article?

Some of what you wrote above may be in the A/B/C/D choices. Look at these now and choose the correct answer.

Part 4

Questions 21–25

Read the text below and questions on the opposite page.
For each question, mark the correct letter **A**, **B**, **C** or **D** on your answer sheet.

It is well known that the building development company Cityspace wants to knock down the existing seafront sports club in Layton and replace it with a leisure centre that will consist of a multi-screen cinema, restaurants and an entertainment centre. But a local action group has promised to fight the £30 million redevelopment of the sports club, which has provided family facilities for over 25 years.

The action group was set up three weeks after the project was announced. Members of the group argue that the new centre will be too big and will totally change the way the town looks. They also dislike the removal of sports facilities from the centre and the change to less healthy activities such as video games and films. Apart from the size of the project, they say that the 550 parking spaces provided will be too few and parking will become more difficult as a result.

Local hotel owners have welcomed the project, but the action group says that in general it will only have a bad effect on the neighbourhood. According to one group member it will result in up to 4,000 people being around Layton seafront late at night. 'A lot of old people and families live nearby,' he explained. A meeting is being held tonight to discuss the plans.

21 What is the writer trying to do in the article?

   A show why the new leisure centre is needed

   B give her own opinion about the new leisure centre

   C describe the arguments against the new leisure centre

   D suggest where the new leisure centre should be built

22 What will the reader discover from the article?

   A how long it will take to complete the new leisure centre

   B how many members the action group has

   C how much it will cost to join the new leisure centre

   D how long the sports club has been in Layton

23 What does the action group think about the new leisure centre?

   A It will not be right for the area.

   B It will cost too much to build.

   C It will not attract enough people.

   D It will provide too little entertainment.

24 Which group of people is keen on having the new leisure centre?

   A people who do a lot of sport

   B people working in the tourist industry

   C people who come into Layton by car

   D people living near the seafront

25 What would be a good headline for the article?

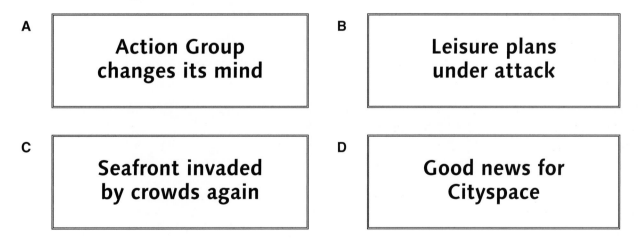

A Action Group changes its mind	**B** Leisure plans under attack
C Seafront invaded by crowds again	**D** Good news for Cityspace

TIP

Read through the whole text first for general understanding. Don't worry about choosing the A, B, C, D answers yet.

Look at the title. You might not know anything about James Cook, but the text will be some sort of biography.

Look at the example that is given. Write the answer in the space (0). The first sentence gives you important information. It's like a summary of what you're going to read.

Now read the text, but don't look at the A/B/C/D choices.

1 What was James Cook's job?

2 What good thing did he do for the sailors on the ship, *Endeavour*?

3 Which different places did he visit?

Read the text again and choose the correct word for each space.

When you've finished, look at questions 26–35 again. Most of the questions test vocabulary, but try to find an example of the following:
– a prepositional phrase
– a pronoun
– a quantity adjective
– a 'time' word.

Part 5

Questions 26–35

Read the text below and choose the correct word for each space.
For each question, mark the correct letter **A**, **B**, **C** or **D** on your answer sheet.

Example:

| 0 | **A** became | **B** changed | **C** reached | **D** earned | ***Answer:*** | 0 | A ▬ | B ☐ | C ☐ | D ☐ |

James Cook

James Cook sailed around the world in the late 18th century and **(0)** .... famous as an explorer.
He first went to sea in 1746. Eleven years later, he **(26)** .... the navy. He was a very good sailor
and **(27)** .... was not long before he was given his own ship.

In 1768, the Royal Society **(28)** .... a scientific voyage to Tahiti. Cook was asked to command
the ship, *Endeavour*, and to take a group of scientists **(29)** .... board. The voyage lasted three years.
Cook made **(30)** .... that his sailors ate fresh fruit. In this way, he was able to **(31)** .... them
from the terrible illnesses **(32)** .... by a bad diet.

Cook was the first European to draw maps of New Zealand and to **(33)** .... eastern Australia.
He also sailed to Antarctica and drew maps of the Pacific and its **(34)** .... islands. In 1779, he died
(35) .... a fight in Hawaii.

26	**A** connected	**B** met	**C** joined	**D** added
27	**A** there	**B** it	**C** that	**D** he
28	**A** developed	**B** fetched	**C** organised	**D** performed
29	**A** at	**B** on	**C** for	**D** with
30	**A** true	**B** real	**C** exact	**D** sure
31	**A** avoid	**B** mind	**C** save	**D** help
32	**A** caused	**B** supplied	**C** appeared	**D** happened
33	**A** realise	**B** know	**C** learn	**D** discover
34	**A** most	**B** more	**C** much	**D** many
35	**A** while	**B** during	**C** since	**D** until

Write a maximum of three words to complete each sentence. You will lose the mark if you write an answer longer than three words, even if it includes the correct answer.

In this part of the Writing Test, you are asked to complete a second sentence so that it means the same as the first. This part tests grammatical structures.

Look at the questions opposite. They are all about a new shopping centre.

Question 1

Look at the <u>underlined</u> words in the first sentence. This is the structure you have to focus on (present perfect). Look at the gapped sentence. The ending says 'a week ago'.

1   What tense usually goes with 'ago'?
    a) present perfect   b) past simple

Now complete question 1.

Question 2

Read both parts of question 2.

2   <u>Underline</u> the word in the first sentence that you need to focus on.

3   Which of these three forms fits with 'It took us half an hour'?
    a) to drive   b) driving   c) drive

Now complete question 2.

Question 3

4   Which preposition is needed here?
    a) of   b) in   c) outside

Now complete question 3.

Question 4

The first sentence tells you why you got lost.

5   Which 'joining word' tells you why something happened?
    a) although   b) but   c) because

Now complete question 4.

Question 5

6   When did you leave the centre?
    a) at 4.30 p.m.   b) before 4.30 p.m.

7   The first sentence tells you *exactly* when 'we left the centre'. The second sentence begins with a negative structure – 'We didn't leave …' Choose the correct word to continue this sentence.
    a) before   b) until   c) at

Now complete question 5.

Part 1

Questions 1–5

Here are some sentences about a new shopping centre.
For each question, complete the second sentence so that it means the same as the first.
Use no more than three words. Write only the missing words on your answer sheet.
You may use this page for any rough work.

Example:
Our trip to the new shopping centre was enjoyable.
We ...*enjoyed*... our trip to the new shopping centre.   ***Answer:*** | 0 | *enjoyed* |

---

1   The new shopping centre <u>has been open for a week</u>.

   The new shopping centre .... **a week ago.**

2   We spent half an hour driving to the centre.

   It took us half an hour .... **to the centre.**

3   The car park had five lifts.

   There were five lifts .... **the car park.**

4   The first shop was so big that we got lost in it.

   We got lost in the first shop .... **it was so big.**

5   It was 4.30 p.m. when we left the centre.

   We didn't leave the centre .... **4.30 p.m.**

TIP

Make sure you address your message to the person named in the instructions, and write your name at the end of the message.

First, read question 6 below.

Now read this student's answer.

> Dear Tim,
> I would like to come to the concert with you, but I'm sorry. I have to go to see my grandfather on Saturday. So, would you want to go dancing next Saturday? I'll phone you as soon as I arrive.
>
> Faithfully Ibrahima

Underline the words that Ibrahima uses to:
- apologise
- explain why she can't go
- suggest something they can do together the following weekend.

This message was awarded a Band 5 – top marks (see page 9 for the General Mark Scheme). The examiner's comments were:

> 'In this answer all three content elements are covered and the message is clearly communicated.'

Now read another student's answer to the *same* question.

> Dear Tim, I can't go with you to a concert this Saturday. I'm very ill. I have got a flu. But I'm going with you as soon as possible. I think it will be a next week. Pleas call me on Friday. I will be able to tell you, what I feel. I'd like to take with us my husband, too.
>
> Your Jane

Underline the words that Jane uses to explain why she can't go to the concert.

The examiner's comments were:

> 'Only one content element (the reason) is covered satisfactorily; there is no apology and no clear suggestion for another meeting.'

This answer received a Band 2.

Use the beginning of Jane's message from 'Dear Tim' to '… very ill'. Rewrite the rest of the message to include the other two points.

Part 2

Question 6

Tim, an English friend of yours, has asked you to go to a concert with him this Saturday, but you cannot go.

Write an email to Tim. In your email, you should
- apologise
- explain why you cannot go
- suggest something you can do together the following weekend.

Write **35–45 words** on your answer sheet.

TIP

Allow about 20–25 minutes to write your story or letter.

Read question 7 below. Before you write the letter, think about what you're going to say:

- What's your penfriend's name?
- What's the name of the video?
- What's it about?
- Why would your penfriend like it?

Think about the closing sentence for your letter.

Now, write your letter in about 100 words.

Read question 8 below. Before you write your story, think about what you're going to say:

- Why was it the most important day of your life?
- What happened?
- How did you feel?
- Did it work out well or badly in the end?

Now, write your story in about 100 words.
What verb tense(s) will you use for your story?

Part 3

Write an answer to **one** of the questions (**7** or **8**) in this part.
Write your answer in about **100 words** on your answer sheet.
Mark the question number in the box at the top of your answer sheet.

Question 7

- This is part of a letter you receive from an English penfriend.

> *I've just got a new video recorder and want to buy some videos. What's the best video you have seen recently? Do you think I'd like it?*

- Now write a letter, answering your penfriend's questions.
- Write your **letter** on your answer sheet.

Question 8

- Your English teacher has asked you to write a story.
- Your story must begin with this sentence.

I woke up knowing it was the most important day of my life.

- Write your **story** on your answer sheet.

Listening • PART 1

TIP

The extracts in Part 1 are very short so don't worry if you can't answer first time. Everything is played twice.

In the exam, you have to look at the question and the pictures quickly (five seconds). In your mind, you'll probably notice the difference in the pictures.

Read questions 1–7 in the exam and look at the suggestions/questions in this section *before* you listen to the recording.

Question 1

How many people are in each picture and where are they? For example, in A there are two people on the beach.

Question 2

Write the times above the pictures, e.g. A is 9.15.

Question 3

What are the four different objects in the pictures?

Question 4

Think quickly what each picture represents, e.g. A is a picnic by the sea.

Question 5

How many different objects are shown?

Question 6

What are the three methods of transport in the pictures?

Question 7

What are the three ways of making music?

Now listen to the recording and answer questions 1–7.

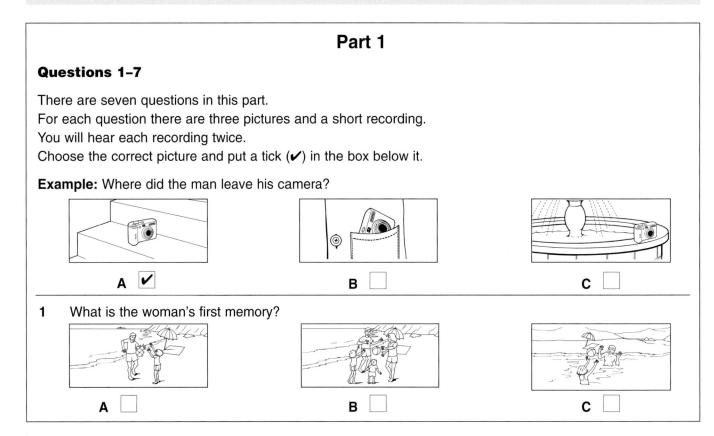

Part 1

Questions 1–7

There are seven questions in this part.
For each question there are three pictures and a short recording.
You will hear each recording twice.
Choose the correct picture and put a tick (✔) in the box below it.

Example: Where did the man leave his camera?

A ✔   B ☐   C ☐

1 What is the woman's first memory?

A ☐   B ☐   C ☐

2 Which train will the woman catch?

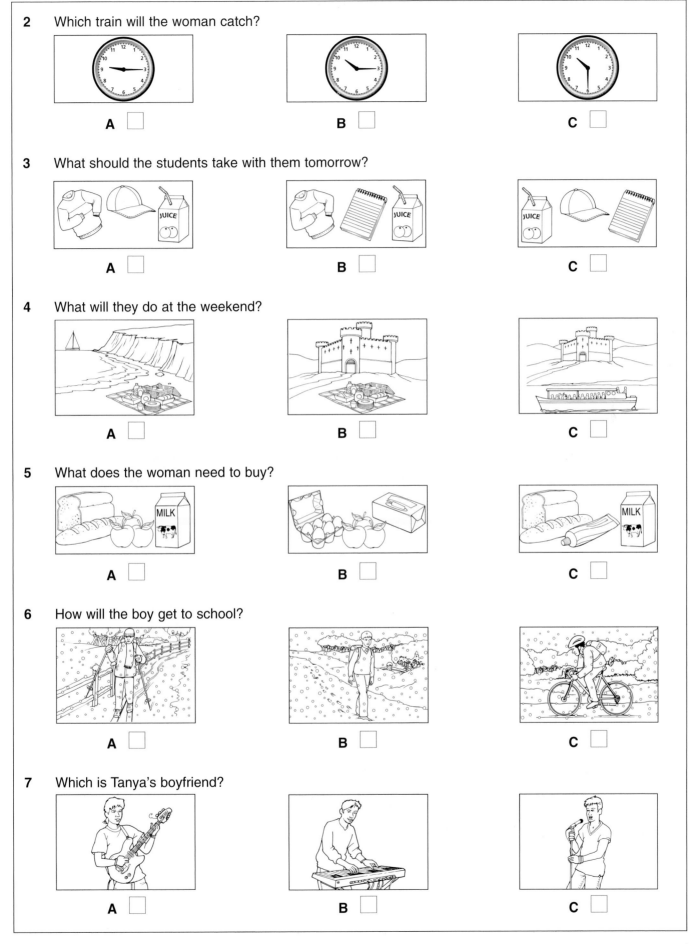

A ☐   B ☐   C ☐

3 What should the students take with them tomorrow?

A ☐   B ☐   C ☐

4 What will they do at the weekend?

A ☐   B ☐   C ☐

5 What does the woman need to buy?

A ☐   B ☐   C ☐

6 How will the boy get to school?

A ☐   B ☐   C ☐

7 Which is Tanya's boyfriend?

A ☐   B ☐   C ☐

TIP

You have 45 seconds to read the questions before your hear the recording. Remember the questions are in the same order as the information on the recording.

For this exercise, don't look at the questions opposite yet.

Listen once to the recording. You will hear a teacher talking to a group of students.

Write down six topic areas that you think the questions will focus on, for example:

1 _Sam's Disco_ ....

2 ....

3 ....

4 ....

5 ....

6 ....

Now look at questions 8–13 opposite. Do any of them match the topic areas you wrote down?

Listen to the recording again and choose the correct answers.

Part 2

You will hear a teacher talking to a group of students.
For each question, put a tick (✔) in the correct box.

---

8 Why is tonight's disco special?

A ☐ It's the last week of the course.

B ☐ It's Sam's birthday.

C ☐ It starts earlier than usual.

9 Where will the football match take place?

A ☐ at Henry's College

B ☐ at the sports centre

C ☐ in a park

10 After the football match, the students will

A ☐ go to a pizza restaurant.

B ☐ have a party at the college.

C ☐ celebrate on the beach.

11 The train to Thornton leaves at

A ☐ 12.15.

B ☐ 12.45.

C ☐ 1.20.

12 What should the students bring to the picnic?

A ☐ drinks

B ☐ bread rolls

C ☐ glasses

13 What does the teacher suggest they do at the lake?

A ☐ go fishing

B ☐ go for a walk

C ☐ take photos

TIP

All the words that you need to write in the numbered spaces will be heard on the recording.

Read the instructions and questions 14–19 below. Before you listen, look at the following suggestions and questions:

Question 14

You can write the number in full or you can put it in figures.

Question 15

You hear about a few different businesses, but only one is run by the woman.

Question 16

Do you think the missing word will be in the singular or plural form?

Question 17

Give an example of something that you could write in this space.

Questions 18 and 19

You just need one word for each answer.

Listen to the recording and fill in the missing information for questions 14–19.

Listen again and check your answers.

Part 3

Questions 14–19

You will hear someone who lives in Lidsey talking on the radio.
For each question, fill in the missing information in the numbered space.

LIDSEY

Number of people who live there: **(14)** ....

Type of business the woman runs: **(15)** ....

Food grown locally: potatoes and **(16)** ....

A local company makes **(17)** ....

Tourist attractions: **(18)** ....

(19) ....

TIP

Read the instructions. You'll learn who the speakers are and what they're talking about before you start to listen. The speakers will give opinions and will agree and disagree with each other.

Listen to the recording and tick which you hear.

1   a) Every time I turn it on … ☐

   b) I've never used the computer before … ☐

2   a) … there seems to be another problem. ☐

   b) … the computer works very well. ☐

3   a) It's easy to learn things when you're an adult. ☐

   b) It's easy to learn things when you're a child. ☐

4   a) I can understand them. ☐

   b) I don't find them easy to follow either. ☐

5   a) I'll try and find a class in the evenings. ☐

   b) I'm too old to go to computer classes. ☐

6   a) … I know about teaching computer skills in schools in different countries. ☐

   b) … this has given me an idea for a special report I have to do. ☐

Now match the ones you have ticked with statements 20–25. Underline the important words.

Part 4

Questions 20–25

Look at the six sentences for this part.
You will hear a conversation between a girl, Mary, and her father, about computers.
Decide if each sentence is correct or incorrect.
If it is correct, put a tick (✔) in the box under **A** for **YES**. If it is not correct, put a tick (✔) in the box under **B** for **NO**.

		A YES	B NO
20	This is the first time that Mary's father has used the computer.	☐	☐
21	There is a fault with the computer.	☐	☐
22	Mary thinks people learn new skills best when they're young.	☐	☐
23	Mary and her father agree that the instructions are badly written.	☐	☐
24	Mary's father is persuaded to go to computer classes.	☐	☐
25	Mary knows a lot about computer teaching in different countries.	☐	☐

Speaking ● PART 1

TIP

> At the beginning of the Speaking Test, the examiner will ask you your name and where you come from. Keep your answers short at this stage of the test.

In the first part of the Speaking Test you will be asked to spell your surname. Practise spelling in English. Spell out loud these surnames:

G-o-n-z-a-l-e-z   L-o-u-b-a-n-i-s

B-a-s-h-i-r   M-a-k-a-y-a-m-a

K-a-u-ff-m-a-nn

Now spell your own surname. Do it a few times until you feel comfortable doing it.

Speaking ● PART 2

TIP

> In this part of the Speaking Test, turn towards your partner and speak to him/her, not the examiner.

Read what the examiner will say to you in Part 2, and look at the ideas on the Picture Sheet on page 102. Say something about all six ideas on the sheet.

You will need the following language to help you do this task:

Language box – talking about 'needs'

This is good because …
He'll probably need … because …
He'll definitely need … because …
I don't think … is so important because …
For me, the most important thing is …
   because …

Part 2 (2–3 minutes)

Interlocutor: *Say to both candidates:*

> I'm going to describe a situation to you.
> A student from **another country** is coming to study **here**. He has asked you what he should **bring**. Talk together about the things he will **need** and say which will be the most **useful**.
> Here is a picture with some ideas to help you.
> *Indicate the **Picture Sheet** on page 102 to the candidates.*
> I'll say that again.
> A student from **another country** is coming to study **here**. He has asked you what he should **bring**. Talk together about the things he will **need** and say which will be the most **useful**.
> All right? Talk together.
> *Allow the candidates enough time to complete the task without intervention. Prompt only if necessary.*
> Thank you.

Speaking ● PARTS 3 AND 4

TIP

> If you don't understand the instructions, ask the examiner to repeat them e.g. 'Sorry, could you say that again, please?'

PART 3

Read what the examiner will say to you in Part 3. You have approximately one minute to say what you can see in the photograph.

Language box

I can see …
There's a … / There are some …
The (woman) is holding/giving, etc.
The woman has (got) blond hair.

Below is a description of photograph 1 on page 103. Complete the description. Use the structures in the language box and any other words that are necessary.

'I can ....*see*....... a family and ....
.... in the kitchen. I think they're
.... breakfast. .... are three children, their parents and grandparents. The man .... some orange juice. The grandmother .... some jam on the bread. I think she's going to give it to one of the children. The grandfather .... an egg for his breakfast. The kitchen .... quite modern. I .... a microwave .... the woman. I think the children are ready for school.'

Look at photograph 2 on page 103. You have about one minute to say what you can see in the photograph.

PART 4

Read what the examiner will say to you in Part 4. It would be very boring if you just gave a list of things you like to do with your family, e.g. eat, go for walks, etc.

It would be more interesting if you added some detail, e.g.

I like having dinner with my family because that's the time we can talk together and tell each other about our days.

Think of some things you like doing with your family, and some things you like doing with your friends.

Practise adding some details, like the example above.

Part 3 (3 minutes)

Interlocutor: *Say to both candidates:*
  Now, I'd like each of you to talk on your own about something. I'm going to give each of you a photograph of **families** spending time together.
  Candidate A, here is your photograph. *(Indicate photograph 1 on page 103.)* Please show it to Candidate B, but I'd like you to talk about it. Candidate B, you just listen, I'll give you your photograph in a moment.
  Candidate A, please tell us what you can see in your photograph.

Candidate A: *Approximately one minute.*
  If there is a need to intervene, prompts rather than direct questions should be used.
  Thank you.

Interlocutor: Now, Candidate B, here is your photograph. It also shows a **family** spending time together. *(Indicate photograph 2 on page 103 to Candidate B.)* Please show it to Candidate A and tell us what you can see in the photograph.

Candidate B: *Approximately one minute.*
  Thank you.

Part 4 (3 minutes)

Interlocutor: *Say to both candidates:*
  Your photographs showed **families** spending time together. Now, I'd like you to talk together about the things **you** like to do with your families, and the things you prefer to do with your **friends**.
  Allow the candidates enough time to complete the task without intervention. Prompt only if necessary.
  Thank you. That's the end of the test.

TEST 2

Reading ● PART 1

TIP

When you look at the notices and messages, think about how you might say them to a friend.

Look at each notice or message opposite. Don't look at the A/B/C choices. Think about how you can say the information in another way.

Question 1

1 Is this notice about
   A problems you might have?
   B problems another swimmer might have?

2 Say it another way. Complete the gaps:
   'see' = *notice*
   'inform' = ...

Now look at the A/B/C choices and circle your answer.

Question 2

1 What is Michael doing when he says 'Don't forget to …'?
   A telling Louise some new information
   B reminding her to do something
   C recommending her to watch something on TV

Now look at the A/B/C choices and circle your answer.

Question 3

1 Is this notice important for
   A all passengers?
   B passengers with bicycles?

2 Say it another way. Complete the gaps:
   'busy periods' = when the train ....
   ....

3 'you cannot bring bicycles onto this train without making a reservation' = you ....
   make a reservation if you want to bring bicycles onto this train.

Now look at the A/B/C choices and circle your answer.

Question 4

Write the names of the four people mentioned in the message.

1 .... ✔ ✘
2 .... ✔ ✘
3 .... ✔ ✘
4 .... ✔ ✘

Look at each person in turn, and decide if they are playing or not. Circle ✔ or ✘.

Now look at the A/B/C choices and circle your answer.

Question 5

1 Why do you think the shop wants to see the customers' repair forms?
   A to prove they have paid
   B to prove the computer belongs to them

2 Now try saying it another way. Complete the gaps:
   The shop .... customers to ....
   a copy of the repair form at the time they
   .... their computer.

Now look at the A/B/C choices and circle your answer.

Part 1

Look at the text in each question.
What does it say?
Mark the correct letter **A**, **B**, or **C** on your answer sheet.

Example:

0

REGENCY CAMERAS
Buy two films
and get one
FREE

A Buy three films for the price of two.

B Get a free film with every one you buy.

C Films bought here are printed free.

Answer: | 0 | A | B | C |

1

Swimming Pool
If you see a person
in difficulty, inform
a member of staff

A If you have difficulty swimming, inform a member of staff before entering the pool.

B Tell a staff member if you notice someone is in danger.

C This pool is for the use of confident swimmers only.

2

Louise,
Before you go out, don't forget to video the science fiction film tonight. It comes on after the six o'clock news.
Thanks,
Michael

Why has Michael written this note?

A to remind Louise to tape a film for him tonight

B to recommend a film for Louise to watch tonight

C to ask Louise to return the video he borrowed

3

PASSENGERS CANNOT BRING
BICYCLES ONTO THIS TRAIN
DURING BUSY PERIODS WITHOUT
MAKING A RESERVATION

A As this train is busy, all passengers must book before boarding.

B Passengers must book before bringing bicycles onto the train at certain times.

C There is no room for bicycles on this train when it is busy.

4

MESSAGE
Greg,
Dave rang. Kim's injured, so Ben needs you to play in Friday's match after all. He's not playing but Dave is, so he'll take you.

Who is going to play in Friday's match?

A Greg and Kim

B Greg and Ben

C Greg and Dave

5

Customers are requested
to produce their copy of
the repair form when
collecting computers

A We want to see a copy of the repair form before we return your computer.

B Customers should fill in a form before leaving their computer for repair.

C Copies of original repair forms are available if requested.

TIP

Remember, there are three extra texts that do not match with any of the people.

It's important to be clear about what the people want, before you read the texts.

Read the instructions and the information about the people (6–10). Complete this grid. If there is no information given for some points, draw a line —.

Now read Text A Beckford, and <u>underline</u> what it offers. Only underline information about subjects offered, age of college, etc. (the categories in the grid below).

Look at the grid you completed. Is there a good match between a person and this college?

Do the same with the other texts.

	subject/career?	old/new college? sports?	country/city?	part-time/full-time?	accommodation
Maria	doctor	older	—	—	college to provide
Henry					
Anna					
Philip					
Monica					

Part 2

Questions 6–10

The people below all want to do a college course.
On the opposite page there are descriptions of eight colleges.
Decide which college would be the most suitable for the following people.
For Questions **6–10**, mark the correct letter (**A–H**) on your answer sheet.

---

6 Maria is 19 years old and wants to qualify as a doctor. She wants to attend an older college and it is important to her that the college also provides accommodation.

7 Henry is a 20-year-old who would like to do management studies at a modern, city centre college. He is looking for a college that will offer him accommodation for his first year.

8 Anna is a 25-year-old who wants to do a degree course in physics. She would like to attend a college with good sports facilities that is situated in a city centre.

9 Philip is an 18-year-old who would like to prepare for a career in education. He is looking for a modern college in the countryside that offers good sports facilities.

10  Monica is a 30-year-old secretary who wants to study German part-time at college. She is looking for a college with sports facilities but doesn't need accommodation.

College Courses

A   Beckford

This city college has many part-time students and is well-known for its courses in European languages and medicine. All courses last four years instead of the normal three. There is no college accommodation but there are good sports facilities, including a recently built swimming pool, on site.

B   Hartfield

The college, founded in 1798, is situated in beautiful countryside. It offers a range of full and part-time courses and is well-known for its courses in education, languages and physics. There are no sports facilities but accommodation is available for all new students.

C   Alton

This is a new college in the city centre. There are no sports facilities but accommodation is provided on site and is available for all new students. There is a big business school here, offering various management courses, and also a recently built languages department. All courses are full-time.

D   Kingston

The college, which dates from the seventeenth century, is three minutes from the city centre. There are no sports facilities on site, but almost 1,000 student flats are provided by the college. The courses in medicine, physics and management studies are popular with students and are available on a full or part-time basis.

E   Garton

This traditional old college is in beautiful countryside on the west coast and is popular for its wide range of sports facilities. It is well-known for its courses in management studies and science. Most courses are available on a full or part-time basis. All full-time students live on site.

F   Middleton

The college is in the very heart of the city. There is no student accommodation but the college offers an excellent, newly built sports centre. There is a full range of science courses, as well as courses in education and business. All courses are full-time and last three to four years.

G   Hampton

This modern college, in the centre of the city, offers both full and part-time courses. Its courses in modern languages and medicine are very popular. There are no sports facilities on site but over 700 student rooms are available and all first-year students qualify for accommodation.

H   Langford

This college, which was built in the 1990s, is situated in beautiful green fields, five kilometres from Hebden village. It has a large sports centre and offers comfortable student accommodation. It is a popular college, particularly for its teacher training and business courses.

TIP

The information given in the text follows the same order as the questions.

First, read the instructions and sentences 11–20 below about a trip to East Africa, and underline what is important – that is, what you think you'll be looking for when you scan the text.

Before you read the text, think of different ways that these underlined words or phrases might be expressed.

There are six sentences that are incorrect: 13, 14, 15, 17, 18, 20. Read the text opposite to find out why they are wrong. Use the questions below to help you.

Question 13: There are three pieces of information in the sentence that you need to find in the text. Only two are correct according to the text.
Which part do the sentence and text not agree on?

Question 14: What *does* disturb the animals?

Question 15: What words does the text use that makes this sentence wrong?

Question 17: What do you find out about the hotel tennis courts in the summer?

Question 18: Does the text mention that training is necessary for this mountain?

Question 20: What is the minimum age for children on climbing trips?

Part 3

Questions 11–20

Look at the sentences below about a trip to East Africa.
Read the text on the opposite page to decide if each sentence is correct or incorrect.
If it is correct, mark **A** on your answer sheet.
If it is not correct, mark **B** on your answer sheet.

---

11   You can see animals from the air on this trip.

12   You can spend a fortnight at the beach.

13   It is possible to see large numbers of birds on Lake Manyara at sunset.

14   Some animals are frightened when visitors use cameras.

15   You are sure to see all the animals you want.

16   You can go windsurfing from the Indian Ocean Hotel.

17   The hotel tennis courts are closed at certain times of the year.

18   Some training is provided if you decide to climb Mount Kilimanjaro.

19   The smallest number of people required on some tours is two.

20   Children can join the Mount Kilimanjaro trip from the age of ten.

The Trip of a Lifetime

Take a trip to East Africa. You begin this trip by visiting the wonderful wildlife parks. As well as travel by coach, there is also an opportunity to take a short trip in a hot-air balloon over the parks to get a better view of the wildlife.

After visiting the wildlife parks you have the choice of either spending the rest of your holiday (7 nights) climbing Mount Kilimanjaro – the highest mountain in Africa – or, for the not so adventurous, sunbathing on the beautiful white sand beside the Indian Ocean. (It is also possible to stay an extra week at the coast.)

Day One: Fly from London Heathrow to Nairobi, Kenya.

Day Two: Drive to the National Park at Lake Manyara. This park is famous for the large variety of birds, which you can see there early in the morning.

Day Three: Leave Manyara for the Serengeti National Park, where you may see elephants, lions and giraffes.

Days Four to Nine: Spend these days travelling by coach around the park. All visitors have a window seat on the coach with a clear view for photographs of the park and animals. Although the animals are not worried by tourists taking photos, we ask visitors to speak quietly so as not to disturb them too much.

Accommodation in tents is normal in the parks. All have private washing facilities. The tents have plenty of space, are very comfortable and have a solid floor. The guides are highly experienced, but there is always the possibility that you may be very unlucky and not see certain animals.

Day Ten: Departure for the mountain trek or to the Indian Ocean.

The Indian Ocean Hotel is on the beach and all rooms have air-conditioning and sea views. All water sports are available and there are tennis courts, which you can use free of charge except during high season, when there is a small booking fee.

No special skills are needed to climb Mount Kilimanjaro, but if you choose this trip you must already be fit and healthy and ready to accept some very basic accommodation in mountain huts.

Most tours and safaris can only operate with a minimum number of passengers. If this number is not reached, we might cancel the tour. If this happens, we will make a decision at least 8 weeks before departure and will try to arrange a different holiday. Minimum numbers can be from 2 to 15 according to the tour.

For practical reasons, children under the age of 8 (under 12 on climbing holidays) may not be accepted on certain tours.

TIP

With multiple-choice questions, three of the choices are wrong; in the text, you can always find what makes them wrong.

Read the text below and opposite once and answer these general questions:

1 Whose opinions about singing are printed in the article – the writer's or Ruth Black's?
2 Why is England different from most other places?
3 Why don't most people sing? (two reasons)
4 a) According to Ruth Black, what's the main advantage of singing?
   b) What are some of the other advantages?
5 How did Ruth first discover a singing class for herself?
6 Why did she start running her own classes?
7 Are there only professional singers in her classes?

Read the text again.

Now look at questions 21–25 and the A/B/C/D choices. Before you decide on your answer, think about the following:

Question 21

Look very carefully at the verb at the beginning of each choice. Does the *writer* explain, describe, advertise or encourage?

Question 22

All these choices look possible! But if you read carefully you will find some words in the text that lead you to the one right answer. Underline them.

Question 23

This question asks for Ruth's opinion of the main advantage of singing with other people. Underline the words that show you what this will be.

Question 24

'A' looks an attractive answer but it's wrong. Underline the words in the text that give you the correct answer.

Question 25

In order to choose the right answer, you need to think what you know about Ruth's classes. Look at each advertisement.

A Does Ruth want professional singers?   Yes/No
B Did you read anything about a neighbourhood concert?   Yes/No
C Are Ruth's classes for people with and without experience?   Yes/No
D Are Ruth's classes every week?   Yes/No

Choose the correct answers for questions 21–25.

Part 4

Questions 21–25

Read the text and questions below.
For each question, mark the correct letter **A**, **B**, **C** or **D** on your answer sheet.

Imagine if everyone in your street suddenly came out into the road one day and started singing together. Singing teacher Ruth Black believes it would make everyone so friendly that they would never walk past each other again without saying hello.

Singing helps people live in peace together, she says. All over the world people have always sung together and in most places they still do, but in England it is no longer traditional. Nowadays, says Ruth, people only sing together in churches and football grounds, although it could be done anywhere. Everyone is able to sing, she says, but most of us either think we can't or have forgotten what we learned as children.

However, as with everything musical, you need to practise and the same applies to your voice. Ruth believes that singing itself brings other benefits. It encourages good breathing, for example. Through singing, people often become more confident and also learn to control stress. But more than anything, it brings people together.

When Ruth first started singing, there was little opportunity to sing with others. Then, through a friend, she discovered an excellent singing class and became so keen that she started running her own classes. These are held twice a month for all singers, whatever their level, and are now enormously successful.

21 What is the writer trying to do in this article?

  A explain why singing has become less popular everywhere

  B describe a teacher's ideas about the importance of singing

  C advertise a teacher's singing classes

  D encourage children to learn to sing

22 What can the reader find out from the article?

  A how singing is something anyone can do

  B where the best places to learn to sing are

  C why traditional singing has disappeared

  D how to improve your singing voice

23 Ruth believes the main benefit of singing with other people is that

  A you learn to breathe more easily.

  B you are able to improve your speaking.

  C you can get to know other people.

  D you become a confident musician.

24 What made Ruth start her own class?

  A She couldn't find a suitable class.

  B She was asked to teach people she knew.

  C She wanted to improve her own teaching.

  D She enjoyed going to a singing class herself.

25 Which is the best advertisement for Ruth's singing classes?

A
CALLING ALL SINGERS!
Want an opportunity to sing
with others? We need professional
singers to join our group.
Come along.

B
THE SOUND OF MUSIC
Our class wants individual
singers for a neighbourhood
street concert.
Come and join us.

C
SING WITH US
Think you can't sing?
See how you improve with practice!
Our popular class is for singers,
both with and without experience.

D
SONGS FOR ALL!
Can you sing? Try our
'Singing for Everyone' class
every week and find out!
Make new friends.

TIP

The words immediately after the gap are very important. Make sure you read the whole sentence, not just the words before the gap.

Look at the title and write in the example answer that is given in space (0). Read the text. Do not look at the A/B/C/D choices yet.

Now, read the text again and work through Questions 26–35. Use the following hints to help you make the right choice.

Question 26: the verb tells us *the name* of the drink.

Question 27: 'it had pepper in it' is *the reason* why it tasted so strong.

Question 28: think carefully about the structures that go with the different choices. Here the structure is *verb + it + infinitive without to*.

Question 29: only one of the choices goes with *of*.

Question 30: notice the word *to* after the gap.

Question 31: this is a phrasal verb that means '*to change from one thing to another*'.

Question 32: how many things?

Question 33: What always follows *ought* and *have*?

Question 34: the relative pronoun you need is talking about the plant.

Question 35: notice the word *with* after the gap. Which verb needs *with*?

Part 5

Read the text below and choose the correct word for each space.
For each question, mark the correct letter **A**, **B**, **C** or **D** on your answer sheet.

Example:

0	**A** reached	**B** arrived	**C** got	**D** went	***Answer:***	0	A	B	C	D

Chocolate

When the Spanish explorer Cortez **(0)** .... Mexico in the sixteenth century, he found the people there using a drink they **(26)** .... chocolate. It tasted quite strong **(27)** .... it had pepper in it. To **(28)** .... it taste better, the Spanish added sugar to it. When chocolate first came to Europe in the seventeenth century, people started to drink it with milk, **(29)** .... of water. Nowadays, tonnes of chocolate and cocoa are **(30)** .... to factories, where they are turned **(31)** .... many popular sweets and cakes.

(32) .... chocolate and cocoa come from the fruit of the cacao tree. Cacao trees **(33)** .... only be grown in hot countries, as they need a warm climate. Cacao is an American plant, **(34)** .... still grows wild in the northern part of South America. Countries in Central and South America were the first to grow it, but today Africa **(35)** .... the world with the most chocolate.

26	**A** announced	**B** told	**C** called	**D** declared
27	**A** while	**B** because	**C** so	**D** whether
28	**A** let	**B** cause	**C** allow	**D** make
29	**A** apart	**B** except	**C** rather	**D** instead
30	**A** delivered	**B** directed	**C** prepared	**D** produced
31	**A** down	**B** into	**C** off	**D** over
32	**A** Both	**B** Every	**C** Either	**D** Each
33	**A** ought	**B** can	**C** have	**D** might
34	**A** what	**B** which	**C** who	**D** whose
35	**A** brings	**B** fetches	**C** supplies	**D** gives

TIP

You must spell correctly. No marks are given if a word is misspelt.

Think about the kinds of changes you have to make in order to complete the second sentence, for example:

- verb tenses
- positive–negative expressions
- pronouns
- comparison structures.

Find a connection between a phrase from A and a phrase from B.

A	B
not as big as	a year ago
it's not necessary	a few
suggested	you don't need to
I was given	smaller than
not far	the cost
is very popular	I really ought to
how much	why not
it'd be good if	he gave me
since last year	everyone likes
not many	quite near

Now look at the sentences below. Use some of the phrases in the exercise above to help you complete the sentences.

Part 1

Questions 1–5

Here are some sentences about taking photographs.
For each question, complete the second sentence so that it means the same as the first.
Use no more than three words.
Write only the missing words on your answer sheet.
You may use this page for any rough work.

Example:

0   I was given a new camera for my birthday by my uncle.

   My uncle .... **a new camera for my birthday.**

   Answer: | 0 | *gave me* |

---

1   So far, I haven't taken many photographs with it.

   So far, I've only taken a .... **photographs with it.**

2   My uncle asked me if I would show him my photographs.

   My uncle said, 'Please would .... **your photographs?'**

3   He suggested trying a different film.

   He said, 'Why .... **try a different film?'**

4   It would be good if I went on a photography course.

   I really ought .... **on a photography course.**

5   My uncle is finding out how much a two-week course costs.

   My uncle is finding out the .... **a two-week course.**

TIP

Keep to the word limit (35–45 words). If you use too many words, the message will not be clear; too few and you probably haven't included the three points.

Use the following notes to write an email to your friends of between 35 and 45 words. Remember to address your friends by name, and to write your name at the end.

Congratulations: *wonderful news / very happy*

Ask about baby: *name? like Mum or Dad?*

Present: *a toy bear*

First, read question 6 below.

- What's just happened?

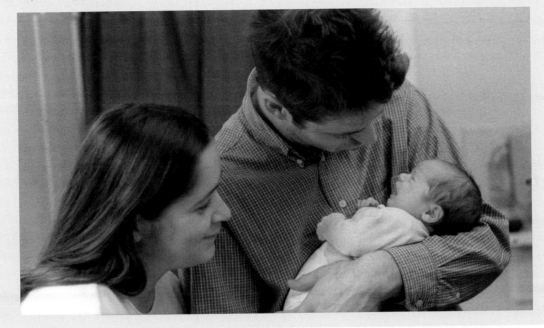

Part 2

Question 6

Some friends in the USA have just had their first baby and you decide to write to them immediately. Write an email to your friends. In your email, you should

- offer them your congratulations
- ask about their baby
- say what present you are sending them.

Write **35–45** words on your answer sheet.

TIP

Don't write a full, rough copy – just make some quick notes to plan your answer.

Read question 7 opposite.

Now, plan what you're going to write.

What is your favourite sport? ....

When do you play it? Who with? ....

How long have you been playing it? ....

Are you any good at it? ....

Why do you like it? ....

Write a letter to your friend (name?) in about 100 words.

Read question 8 opposite.

Getting ideas:

The story begins 'The bus was late so I decided to walk.'

How do you continue? You can get some ideas by asking yourself:

> Where?   Who?
> Why?   What?
> When?   How (long/much/often, etc.)?

For example:

> Where were you going?
> Why were you going there?
> When were you waiting for the bus?
> Who were you with?
> Who did you see during your walk?
> What happened during the walk?
> What was the weather like?
> How long did it take you?

Read a student's answer and the comments which follow.

The bus was late so I decided to walk. That day I had a lesson. During my walk I met my friend Claudia. We didn't meet each other for long time so I decided to go with her in a bar. She was very down because her boyfriend was away for a work. I wanted to help her and so I suggested to go to disco that evening. So we went to Jubilee and she enjoied herself too much. So I was very happy and she too because that evening she met a lot of her old friend and so for few hour didn't remind her boyfriend.

This answer is OK – it has some good parts but it also has some problems, e.g. *I suggested to go to disco.* There is an adequate range of structures and some simple linking, e.g. *During my walk I met my friend.* A number of errors, e.g. *so for few hour didn't remind her boyfriend* make it a bit difficult for the reader to follow. (This answer was given a Band 3 – see page 9 for the Mark Scheme for Writing Part 3.)

Write your ideas for a 100-word story beginning *'The bus was late so I decided to walk.'*

Part 3

Write an answer to **one** of the questions (**7** or **8**) in this part.

Write your answer in about **100 words** on your answer sheet.

Mark the question number in the box at the top of your answer sheet.

Question 7

- This is part of a letter you receive from an English friend.

  I've always wanted to know more about your favourite sport. Tell me all about it. Why do you like it?

- Now write a letter, telling your friend about your favourite sport.
- Write your **letter** on your answer sheet.

Question 8

- Your English teacher has asked you to write a story.
- Your story must begin with this sentence:

  The bus was late so I decided to walk.

- Write your **story** on your answer sheet.

Listening • PART 1

TIP

Look at the questions and pictures and think about what kind of information you are going to hear.

Read the questions in Part 1 and look at the exercise below *before* you listen to the recording. In the exam, you won't have time to write anything but you will be able to notice some important points in either the question or the pictures.

Question 1

There is one very important word in this question. Underline what you think it is.

Question 2

Again, there is one word in this question that you need to concentrate on. Underline it.

Question 3

Look quickly at the three pictures. Where can you see the knife?

Question 4

In pictures B and C, where is the bike and what's happening to the books?

Question 5

What are the three main areas of difference in these pictures?

Question 6

Imagine someone asks you: 'What's the time?' Answer with the times in the pictures.

Question 7

What do the three postcards show?

Now listen to the recording and choose the correct pictures.

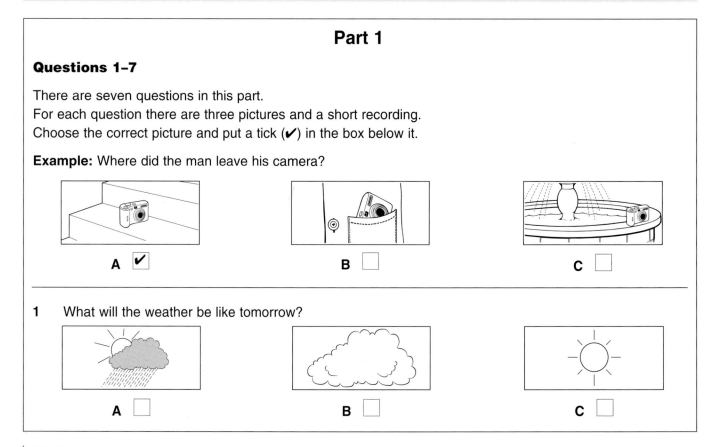

Part 1

Questions 1–7

There are seven questions in this part.
For each question there are three pictures and a short recording.
Choose the correct picture and put a tick (✔) in the box below it.

Example: Where did the man leave his camera?

A ✔   B ☐   C ☐

1   What will the weather be like tomorrow?

A ☐   B ☐   C ☐

2 What will the man do first?

A 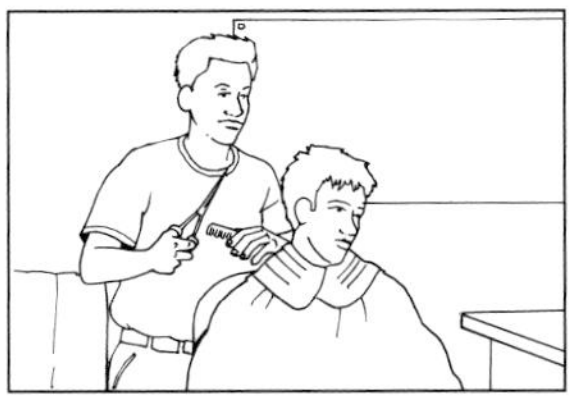 ☐   B  ☐   C ☐

3 Where's the knife?

A  ☐   B  ☐   C ☐

4 What happened to the girl this afternoon?

A  ☐   B  ☐   C ☐

5 Which man is waiting at the bus stop?

A  ☐   B  ☐   C ☐

6 What time does the television programme end?

A  ☐   B  ☐   C ☐

7 Which postcard will they send to Mark?

A  ☐   B  ☐   C ☐

TIP

When you listen to the recording for the first time, answer as many questions as you can. Use the second listening to check your answers and complete any missing answers.

Look at questions 8–13 opposite.

Put a piece of paper over the A/B/C choices so you can't see them, but you can still see the questions.

Listen to the recording *once* and think about how you could answer or complete the questions. Make notes.

Now look at the choices. Then listen again to complete the task. Do any of the answers you wrote down match the choices?

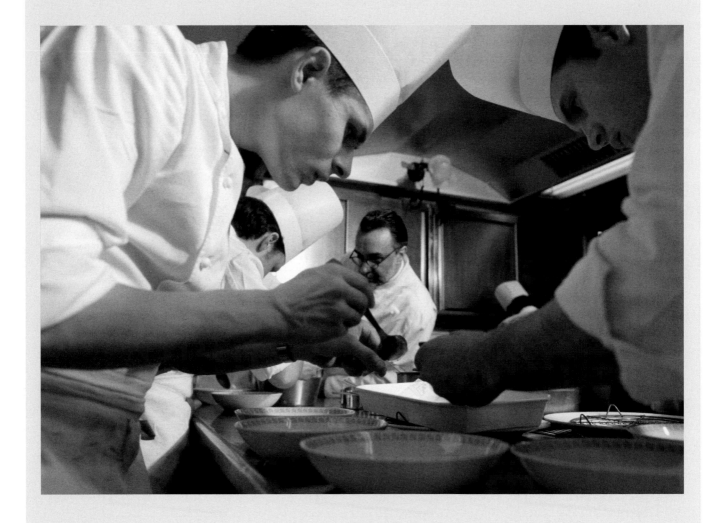

Part 2

You will hear a young man called Toby Wood talking on the radio about what it's like to work in the kitchen of a famous chef.

For each question, put a tick (✔) in the correct box.

---

8 Toby says that working in Oliver Rix's restaurant kitchen was

    A very enjoyable. ☐

    B too hard. ☐

    C very amusing. ☐

9 What was one of Toby's problems in the kitchen?

    A He made too much noise. ☐

    B He couldn't find anything. ☐

    C He prepared too many vegetables. ☐

10 What is important to Oliver about the biscuits?

    A learning to cook them ☐

    B making them look good ☐

    C checking they taste nice ☐

11 Oliver becomes angry when

    A the customers complain. ☐

    B his cooks throw food away. ☐

    C food isn't ready on time. ☐

12 What do the kitchen staff say about Oliver?

    A He should pay them more. ☐

    B He is wrong to shout at them. ☐

    C He teaches them many things. ☐

13 Oliver encourages his young cooks to

    A continue working for him. ☐

    B train with other chefs. ☐

    C learn from each other. ☐

TIP

Usually you don't need to write more than one word or set of figures in each gap.

You're going to listen to someone talking to passengers on a boat from England to France. Look at the questions below.

It is impossible to know exactly what information is missing without listening, but for practice, try writing some possible ideas of your own (in pencil). This will help you feel prepared for the answers when you hear them.

In the exam, you will only have time to *think* of the kind of information that is missing. For example:

Question 14 – write the number of hours the voyage might take.

Now write some ideas for questions 15 to 19.

Listen to the recording. Were the ideas that you wrote before similar to any of the correct answers?

Part 3

Questions 14–19

You will hear someone talking to passengers on a boat from England to France.
For each question, fill in the missing information in the numbered space.

Voyage from Portsmouth to St Malo

Time voyage takes: **(14)** .... hours

Weather forecast: **(15)** ....

In emergency, go to lounge on **(16)** ....

Food: – Lunch and dinner in Ocean Grill

          – **(17)** .... and drinks in Captain's Café

At 3.30, in Children's Play Centre, there's a

          (18) .... show.

Buy stamps in **(19)** ....

TIP

Read the statements carefully and think about the exact meaning of each one.

Read the instructions for Part 4 but don't look at sentences 20–25.

Read questions 1–10 below. Listen to the conversation between Charlotte and her father about what she's going to study next year and answer them.

1 Who believes that Spanish grammar is easy?
2 Why does Charlotte want to study Spanish?
3 Where were Charlotte's great-grandparents born?
4 Where was Charlotte's grandmother born?
5 What stopped Charlotte's father from learning Chinese?
6 How does he feel about this?
7 Charlotte would like to go to China. What worries Charlotte's father about this plan?
8 How many students would there be on the China trip?
9 Does Charlotte think her mother is interested in visiting China?
10 Does Charlotte's father agree with this opinion?

Now, look at sentences 20–25 below.

Listen to the recording again, and decide if the sentences are correct or incorrect.

Part 4

Questions 20–25

Look at the six sentences for this part.
You will hear a conversation between a girl, Charlotte, and her father about what she's going to study next year.
Decide if each sentence is correct or incorrect.
If it is correct, put a tick (✔) in the box under **A** for **YES**. If it is not correct, put a tick (✔) in the box under **B** for NO.

		A YES	B NO
20	Charlotte wants to study Spanish because she thinks Spanish grammar is easy.	☐	☐
21	Charlotte's grandmother was born in England.	☐	☐
22	Charlotte's father is sorry he can't speak Chinese.	☐	☐
23	Charlotte's father is keen on her studying in China.	☐	☐
24	Charlotte plans to go to China alone.	☐	☐
25	Charlotte and her father agree that her mother wants to visit China.	☐	☐

Speaking ● PART 1

TIP

After the first two or three questions (What's your name? Where do you come from?, etc.), you will be asked a question (or two) that requires a longer answer, e.g. why you like something, or some detail about a hobby.

In this part of the test, you may be asked questions about people in your life, for example, family, friends or teachers.
Think what you could say about:

family – brothers / sisters / how many / older or younger? – parents / grandparents
friends – who / what you do together / why you're friends
teachers – what subject / like or dislike / why?

Speaking ● PART 2

TIP

Remember to listen as well as speak.

Read what the examiner will say to you in Part 2 and look at the ideas for a 70th birthday present on the Picture Sheet on page 104. Make sure you interact with your partner.

Language box

Think about how you can start the task:
Shall I start?　　　You go first.
Where shall we start?

Think about how you can get your partner involved.
What about this one?
Do you think he should …?
I don't think this one is very good, do you?
Why don't we …?
I think … . What do you think?
Let's have a look at some other ideas.

Read part of the interaction between two students talking about this task. Do they use any of the language in the box above?

Student 1: So it's a present for his grandmother's 70th birthday.
Student 2: Yes, where shall we start? The bird – I don't think that's so good, maybe she doesn't like birds.
Student 1: No, some people don't. And it needs cleaning and things. What about gloves? Not very exciting, are they?
Student 2: No – flowers are always nice, but they die quickly. I don't think a computer is a good idea, do you? It's too expensive for a teenager to buy for a birthday present.
Student 1: You're right. Maybe he could give her …

If you're working with a partner, finish the task.

Part 2 (2–3 minutes)

Interlocutor: *Say to both candidates:*
I'm going to describe a situation to you.
A teenager wants to give his grandmother a **present** for her seventieth **birthday**. But he doesn't know what to buy. Talk together about the different things he could **give** her and then say which would be most **suitable**.
Here is a picture with some ideas to help you.
*Hand over the **Picture Sheet** on page 104 to the candidates.*
I'll say that again.
A teenager wants to give his grandmother a **present** for her seventieth **birthday**. But he doesn't know what to buy. Talk together about the different things he could **give** her and then say which would be most **suitable**.
All right? Talk together.
Allow the candidates enough time to complete the task without intervention. Prompt only if necessary.
Thank you.

TIP

When your partner is talking about his/her photograph in Part 3, don't interrupt.

PART 3

Read what the examiner will say to you in Part 3.

When you're talking about your photograph, you need to describe what you can see. It isn't necessary to talk about your impressions and opinions but if you want to, here is some language to help you.

Language box

She looks + adjective
e.g. The woman on the left looks cold.

They/He/It could be …
e.g. They could be on holiday.

It/She might be
e.g. It might be in Germany or somewhere like that.

probably
e.g. It's probably winter or springtime.

Maybe
e.g. Maybe they're friends.

Practise with photographs 3 and 4 on page 105. First, say what you can see, then use some of the language from the box above.

PART 4

Read what the examiner will say to you in Part 4.

Read this conversation between two candidates. It is correct but not very interesting.

Student 1: I drink coffee at breakfast and water at lunchtime.
Student 2: Me too. In the evening, for dinner I have wine sometimes, or usually water.
Student 1: Oh, I have coke.
Student 2: I have coke sometimes too.

Can you make it better? Think of your answers to these questions:

● Why do you drink coffee for breakfast?
● Do you like water?
● Are there some drinks you don't like?
● Are there drinks you like when you're doing sport, or when you're hot or cold?
● Do you drink when you're studying? What?

If you're working with a partner, talk together about what you like to drink with your meals and what you drink at other times of the day.

Part 3 (3 minutes)

Interlocutor: *Say to both candidates:*
Now, I'd like each of you to talk on your own about something. I'm going to give each of you a photograph of people having a **drink**.
Candidate A, here is your photograph. *(Indicate photograph 3 on page 105.)* Please show it to Candidate B, but I'd like you to talk about it. Candidate B, you just listen, I'll give you your photograph in a moment.
Candidate A, please tell us what you can see in your photograph.

Candidate A: *Approximately one minute.*
If there is a need to intervene, prompts rather than direct questions should be used.
Thank you.

Interlocutor: Now, Candidate B, here is your photograph. It also shows people having a **drink**. *(Indicate photograph 4 on page 105.)* Please show it to Candidate A and tell us what you can see in the photograph.

Candidate B: *Approximately one minute.*
Thank you.
Retrieve photograph from Candidate B.

Part 4 (3 minutes)

Interlocutor: *Say to both candidates:*
Your photographs showed people having a **drink**. Now, I'd like you to talk together about what you like to drink, with your **meals** and what you drink at other times of the day.
Allow the candidates enough time to complete the task without intervention.
Prompt only if necessary.
Thank you. That's the end of the test.

TEST 3

Reading • PART 1

TIP

Check that the answer you choose means exactly the same as the text.

Look at each text below and opposite and answer the following questions.

Question 1

1 What have you got to do if you want to go to London? (there may be more than one correct answer)
 A pay for the ticket now
 B write your name on the notice
 C write your phone number on the notice
 D speak to Kim

Question 2

2 If the red light is off, can you go in? Yes/No

Question 3

3 Three ingredients are mentioned:
 a) Who bought the sugar?
 b) Where's the butter?
 c) So, what does James need to get?

Question 4

4 Why is the library closed today?
5 Where can you put your library books?
6 Will you have to pay for the returned books?

Question 5

7 What are the staff doing?
8 What should you do?
9 Who can wait here?

Now choose the correct A/B/C answers.

Part 1

Questions 1–5

Look at the text in each question.
What does it say?
Mark the correct letter **A**, **B**, or **C** on your answer sheet.

Example:

0

> **NO BICYCLES**
> **AGAINST GLASS**
> **PLEASE**

A Do not leave your bicycle touching the window.

B Broken glass may damage your bicycle tyres.

C Your bicycle may not be safe here.

Answer:

1

I'm away, but sign here for London trip next Saturday. Please leave a contact number. Nothing to pay until then (coach costs £15).

Kim

If you want to go to London,

A buy a ticket before Saturday.

B go and tell Kim immediately.

C write your phone number here.

2

PHYSICS LABORATORY

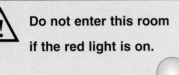 **Do not enter this room if the red light is on.**

A Only come in if there is no red light showing.

B The red light will come on when you enter this room.

C Stay outside until the red light comes on.

3

James,
Have bought some sugar for your biscuits (butter in fridge). Sorry, forgot the flour - get more at Mullin's. Turn oven off afterwards!
Mum

To make biscuits, James needs to buy

A butter.

B flour.

C sugar.

4

LIBRARY CLOSED TODAY BECAUSE OF ILLNESS

NO CHARGE FOR BOOKS RETURNED THROUGH LETTERBOX

A If you are ill, the library will not charge you for returning books late.

B Send any books due back by post, as the library is closed.

C As the library is closed, users can put books through the letterbox.

5

RAIL PASSENGERS WITH TICKETS:

PLEASE QUEUE HERE WHILE OUR STAFF GET YOUR TRAIN READY

A Queue here unless you have already shown your train ticket to our staff.

B Join the queue here to get your train tickets from our staff.

C Wait here with your ticket until staff have prepared your train for boarding.

TIP

A text may look like a good match but does it have **all** the things that the person wants or needs?

Read the information about the people below. <u>Underline</u> what each person is interested in, or wants. The first person has been done for you as an example.

Read each text on page 61 and <u>underline</u> the important information.

Question 6

1 Look at guidebooks F and E.
   Why is one of these not suitable for Keiko?
   e.g. E matches for history but doesn't match for information about inexpensive hotels and public transport. F matches for history, information about towns, hotels and public transport.
   What is the answer to question 6?

Question 7

2 Look at guidebooks D and H.
   Why is one of these not suitable for Dominque?
   What is the answer to question 7?

Question 8

3 Look at guidebooks A and D.
   Why is one of these not suitable for Rachel and John?
   What is the answer to question 8?

Question 9

4 Look at guidebooks B, G and E.
   Why are two of these not suitable for Paolo?
   What is the answer to question 9?

Question 10

5 Look at guidebooks C and B.
   Why is one of these not suitable for Peter and Anna?
   What is the answer to question 10?

Part 2

Questions 6–10

The people below are all looking for a guidebook about Britain.
On the opposite page there are descriptions of eight guidebooks.
Decide which guidebook would be the most suitable for the following people.
For questions **6–10**, mark the correct letter (**A–H**) on your answer sheet.

---

6   Keiko is interested in the <u>history of Britain</u>. She wants to <u>visit</u> as many <u>old cities</u> as she can and needs lists of <u>inexpensive hotels</u>, as well as information about <u>public transport</u>.

7 Dominique is an art student who is interested in seeing the most important art galleries in Britain. She needs to find out how to get to them by train and bus.

8   Rachel and John often visit different parts of Britain. They want information about the best hotels and some advice on where to go out and enjoy themselves in the evenings.

9 Paolo wants to spend time in the countryside and go walking. He needs to find out about inexpensive accommodation. He does not have a car.

10  Peter and Anna have visited the main British tourist centres before, so they now want to see the less popular towns and cities. They have lots of time and would like information on which quiet country roads to use.

Guidebooks on Britain

A This book is for travellers who have money to spend – top-quality hotels are listed, as well as excellent restaurants, shops, theatres, cinemas and nightclubs. Colour maps and photographs of Britain's most important city centres make it an attractive and useful publication.

B If you would like to know more about Britain's history but are tired of museums, this book will take you on a tour of the British countryside, stopping at castles and historical sites. For keen walkers, there are suggested routes, but a car is necessary to reach the start of each one.

C This author stays away from the main tourist centres, which are well covered in other books. He tells us instead about the many towns and villages which are usually forgotten but are certainly worth visiting. His suggested routes avoiding the busy motorways give a wonderful opportunity to drive through the beautiful countryside.

D This is a useful little book giving ideas of things to do during a holiday in Britain. All the most important museums and art galleries are listed. The main entertainment centres – theatres, ballet, opera and music of all kinds – are also covered.

E This book contains a short history of Britain and it is very well done in so few pages. It is illustrated with lots of beautiful colour photographs of both cities and countryside, and also suggests some pleasant areas for walks. There is little practical information for the traveller, however.

F The author covers the history of a number of important British cities and also provides practical information about each one, including names of hotels in every price range. The train and bus information may go out of date very quickly but phone numbers are provided so routes can be checked.

G This book contains 100 walks through fields and forests in five different parts of the country. Every walk starts from a town or city, and some walks can be completed in a day. On others you need to stay somewhere overnight. However, suggestions of reasonably-priced places to stay on the routes are included, as well as information about where to eat and public transport.

H This new book gives useful information on galleries and museums. Unusually, it includes not just the main cities but also suggests visiting smaller towns whose museums and art galleries contain valuable collections. At the back, there is useful advice on using public transport to travel around Britain.

TIP

Do not read the text in detail. Identify what you need to find out and scan the text for that information.

Read sentences 11–20 in Part 3 about a mobile phone service. Underline what is important – that is, what you will need to look for when you scan the text.

Read the text opposite and answer the following questions. Then make your decision – are sentences 11–20 in Part 3 below correct or incorrect?

Question 11

Is there information in the text about 'increasing in size'?

Question 12

The figure 85% is mentioned in the text. What about the words 'more than'?

Question 13

The sentence says '… was better than that of other …'. What words express this in the text?

Question 14

Do Encel need to know what credit card you'll use?

Question 15

Is there a match in the text for all three pieces of information (minimum charge/read a message/5p)?

Question 16

According to the text, how much does 1 minute cost? Does it cost more if you speak for longer e.g. 1 minute 10 seconds?

Question 17

The sentence says '… to help you remember when …' . Is there a match for this in the text?

Question 18

Two pieces of information need to be found (… to record a different message … /… at any time).

Question 19

Why would you need to call 234? What happens when you call 234?

Question 20

With Encel, is there one, or more than one, time period when calls are cheaper? Can *you* choose when you make your cheap calls?

Part 3

Questions 11–20

Look at the sentences below about a mobile phone service.

Read the text on the opposite page to decide if each sentence is correct or incorrect.

If it is correct, mark **A** on your answer sheet.

If it is not correct, mark **B** on your answer sheet.

---

11 The Encel mobile phone network is increasing in size.

12 You can contact more than 85% of people living in the UK on your Encel phone.

13 When asked, people thought that Encel's service was better than that of other companies.

14 You should inform Encel which credit card you will pay for your calls with.

15 The minimum charge to read a text message sent to you is 5p.

16 If your 166 call lasts between one and two minutes, you will be charged 20p.

17 Encel provides a service to help you remember when certain things are happening.

18 It is possible to record a different message on your Encel answerphone at any time.

19 You can learn how to record messages on your answerphone by calling 234.

20 The time period when call charges are at their lowest is fixed by Encel.

Information for new Encel customers

Welcome to Encel, one of the fastest-growing mobile phone networks in the UK. You can go almost anywhere in the UK and use your Encel phone. Our service now reaches up to 85% of the UK population. With Encel you have total freedom and can talk, take messages or send a text message practically anywhere, at any time.

In a recent questionnaire about mobile phone networks, people voted Encel the top service provider in the country. We take our customers seriously and intend to ensure that everyone receives the service they expect.

The easiest way to buy talk time on your phone is by credit card. If you haven't done so already, please let us know which card you'll be using. Then, whenever you need talk time, call 440, free of charge, and tell us the amount you want to buy. If you do not want to use your credit card, vouchers are available from many stores.

You can also send text messages with Encel phones. These are a quick and inexpensive way to contact friends. They are perfect for when talking is difficult – when the music is too loud or when you want to keep something private. Sending a message costs as little as 5p but receiving one is free.

Encel also provides an information service for its mobile phone users. This service gives you recorded information, 24 hours a day, on sport (all the news, plus the day's football and rugby results), weather and finance. Just call 166 from your Encel phone. Calls cost 20p per minute at all times and are charged by the second.

With Encel you can also receive text messages to remind you of important dates. When you register with Encel, you should enter your diary dates, for example friends' birthdays, into a personal calendar. You will then receive a text message, with plenty of time to spare, as a reminder.

The answerphone service provided by Encel includes a facility for you to record a message. It's also possible to change your message whenever you like, so you can let people know exactly what you're doing. To record a message on your Encel answerphone, just dial 234 and follow the instructions. When callers have left messages, it costs just 10p per minute to hear them.

The cost of a call depends on the time of day that you make it. It is normally cheaper to make calls between 6.00 p.m. and 6.00 a.m. However, with Encel, it is possible to choose a different period. You have the choice of morning hours (7.00 a.m.–11.00 a.m.); lunchtime (11.00 a.m.–3.00 p.m.); or afternoon (3.00 p.m.–7.00 p.m.).

TIP

Some of the questions in Part 4 are based on understanding of the whole text. This means that you usually have to look in more than one place in the text to find the answer.

Read the text below.

General questions after first reading:

1 At the beginning, what two things did Colin do with the money he won?
2 What did he plan to do with the rest of the money?
3 Did he believe he had enough money to buy the violin?
4 What happened when he first played the violin?
5 Did his wife criticise him for buying the violin?
6 Why does his wife think he did the right thing?
7 Has Colin retired or is he still playing?

Now read the text again.

Now look at questions 21–25 and the A/B/C/D choices. Before you decide your answer, think about the following:

Question 21

A Does the writer advise or just tell us about a competition?
B Do we know *why* Colin spent a lot of money?
C Does the writer *describe* how or does he just tell us Colin did this?
D Where does the writer *persuade* people?

Question 22

B & D Are we told *how much* money is/was needed?

Question 23

A, B & C Does his wife actually say any of these things about him or the money he won?

Question 24

Look carefully at the question: '*first* found' are important words. B is attractive, but is there anything in the text that says this?

Question 25

A Is there anything in the text about *a record company*?
B Did Colin make an *announcement*?
C Did he *win* the violin in a competition?

Part 4

Questions 21–25

Read the text and questions below.
For each question, mark the correct letter **A**, **B**, **C** or **D** on your answer sheet.

When musician Colin Baker won five hundred thousand pounds in a competition, it seemed the answer to his dreams. Almost immediately, he bought a house and made his own CD recording of some classical music. He intended to save the rest of his money and retire, even though he was only in his late forties.

Then he saw a violin in a shop. It was of such high quality that even top professional players are rarely able to afford one like it. 'I'd never felt money was important until then,' he explained. 'Even with the money I'd won, I wasn't sure I could afford to buy the violin, so I started to leave the shop. Then I thought I'd just try it, and I fell in love with the beautiful sound it made. I knew it was perfect both for live concerts and for recordings.'

Now all the money has gone. 'My wife can't have the study room I promised her, and I can't retire,' says Colin, 'but it doesn't matter.' His wife says, 'I sometimes wish he was more responsible with money, but I'm still pleased for him. I've always helped him in his career, as he's helped me, by sharing everything. We weren't unhappy with our jobs, so we didn't really need the money to escape, and although Colin considered retiring, I know he wouldn't be happy doing that – he loves music too much. I think he did the right thing.'

21 What is the writer trying to do in the text?

    A advise musicians to enter competitions

    B explain why someone spent a lot of money

    C describe how someone got a CD recorded

    D persuade people to prepare for retirement

22 What can a reader learn from the text?

    A how one man's dream ended unhappily

    B how much was paid for a special violin

    C how one couple support each other

    D how much money musicians need for their music

23 What does Colin's wife say about what he did?

    A She wishes he had used the money differently.

    B She feels she didn't really benefit from the money.

    C She is sorry she has lost her study room.

    D She accepts the decision that he made.

24 When Colin first found the violin, he thought

    A he might not have enough money to buy it.

    B he should not spend all of his money on it.

    C he was not a good enough player to own it.

    D he could not leave the shop without it.

25 What did a local newspaper say about Colin's story?

A

A well-known record company has asked a local musician to record a CD after winning a competition …

B

A local musician today announced he would spend every penny of the money he'd won in a competition …

C

A concert audience heard a local musician give a brilliant performance last night on the violin he'd won in a competition …

D

A local musician has decided to continue his career in music in spite of winning some money in a competition …

TIP

When you've chosen your answer, make sure that the remaining three options don't fit the space.

Look at the text. What do you think of when you read this title?

Read the rubric and the example. Fill in the example answer in space (0). Read the text. Don't look at the choices at all. (It might be a good idea to cover them up.)

Try writing your own words in the gaps. If you've understood the text well, you should be able to do this. Two suggestions to help you follow:

Question 29

Be careful if there is a gap at the beginning of the sentence. It's important to read the *whole* sentence. In this sentence, there is a negative/positive contrast ('conditions were hard' and 'climbers made good …'). You need a word that links a negative and positive clause.

Question 35

The word you need should make the comparison stronger – climbing Everest was hard, but that was nothing compared to filming it.

Now look at the A/B/C/D choices. Have you already written in some correct answers?

Part 5

Questions 26–35

Read the text below and choose the correct word for each space.
For each question, mark the correct letter **A**, **B**, **C** or **D** on your answer sheet.

Example:

0   **A**   had   **B**   has   **C**   was   **D**   did

Answer:

0	A	B	C	D
	▬	▭	▭	▭

Filming Everest

Film-maker David Breashears **(0)** .... already climbed Mount Everest three times when he **(26)** .... to make a film, so that audiences could share his **(27)** ....

He set off on this nine-week adventure the following spring, with his photographic equipment and with six climbers from **(28)** .... the world. **(29)** .... the conditions were hard and dangerous, with temperatures of −40 °C, the climbers made good **(30)** .... Then, when they were just one thousand metres from their goal, there was a terrible **(31)** .... The team didn't give **(32)** .... , however. They hid in a tent on the mountainside until it passed. Thirteen days later they **(33)** .... the top.

'I was so tired that it was **(34)** .... to enjoy our success at first,' said David. 'Climbing Everest is difficult enough but filming made it **(35)** .... harder. I am really proud we did it in the end!'

26	**A**	invited	**B**	decided	**C**	organised	**D**	requested
27	**A**	acts	**B**	events	**C**	occupations	**D**	experiences
28	**A**	along	**B**	above	**C**	about	**D**	around
29	**A**	Although	**B**	Because	**C**	Since	**D**	Unless
30	**A**	improvement	**B**	progress	**C**	increase	**D**	development
31	**A**	climate	**B**	storm	**C**	weather	**D**	air
32	**A**	out	**B**	back	**C**	away	**D**	up
33	**A**	arrived	**B**	landed	**C**	reached	**D**	entered
34	**A**	impossible	**B**	unable	**C**	unfit	**D**	improbable
35	**A**	ever	**B**	more	**C**	even	**D**	as

TIP

Remember you must **not** write more than three words and you may only have to write one or two.

Read the instructions to Part 1. Complete the sentences below, or answer the questions.

Question 1

1 If Madonna was the eldest, then all her brothers and sisters were .... than her.

Now complete question 1.

Question 2

2 Why did she move to New York? ....
she wanted to find singing work.

Now complete question 2.

Question 3

3 Which verb from sentence 1 is needed in sentence 2?

4 Which verb tense is used in sentence 1?

Now complete question 3.

Question 4

5 The missing word in sentence 2 is a noun. What word in the sentence tells you this?

6 What do we call a person who sings?

Now complete question 4.

Question 5

7 In sentence 2, 'than' tells you that you need a comparative. What's the comparative form of 'famous'?

Now complete question 5.

Part 1

Questions 1–5

Here are some sentences about the pop star Madonna.

For each question, complete the second sentence so that it means the same as the first.

Use no more than three words.

Write only the missing words on your answer sheet.

You may use this page for any rough work.

Example:

0   As a child in Michigan, Madonna took ballet and singing lessons.

As a child in Michigan, Madonna took lessons in ballet .... as singing.

Answer: | 0 | as well |

---

1   Madonna was the eldest of eight children.
Madonna had seven .... brothers and sisters.

2   She moved to New York in order to find singing work.
She moved to New York .... she wanted to find singing work.

3   It didn't take her long to become famous.
She .... famous very quickly.

4   She has had a long and successful career in singing.
She has been a successful .... for a long time.

5   Madonna is possibly the most famous woman in the world.
Madonna is possibly .... than any other woman in the world.

TIP

It's necessary to write something about all **three** points. **Two** points is not enough to get good marks.

First, read question 6 below.
Make some brief notes about what you're going to write on the postcard.

- Say something about the gallery.
- Explain why you've chosen this postcard for Chris.
- Ask Chris about the weather in Australia.

Read this answer from a student, Pierre.

Hi Chris
How are you?
I am fine. I am on an art gallery. It is very interesting here. Here are some good pictures of famous people. The pictures are modern and some pictures look like graffiti.
Bye!
Yours Pierre

Look back to the notes you made above. Decide which content points Pierre has and hasn't included. Do you think Pierre's answer is good or not?

Now write your postcard to Chris. Remember to
- include all three points
- write in an informal, friendly way
- use names (Chris and yours).

Part 2

Question 6

You visit an art gallery and buy this postcard.
You decide to send the postcard to your friend Chris, who lives in Australia.

In your postcard, you should

- say something about the art gallery
- explain why you have chosen to send Chris this postcard
- ask Chris about the weather in Australia.

Write **35–45 words** on your answer sheet.

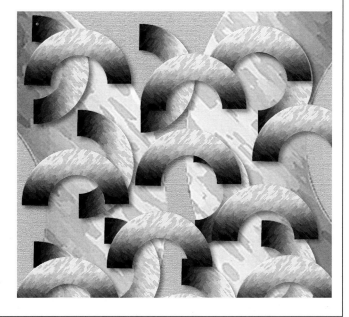

> **TIP**
>
> Make sure your handwriting is clear and easy to read.

Read question 7 opposite.

Organisation: remember to use paragraphs in your letter

Paragraph 1: introductory sentence; say why you're writing

Paragraph 2: give the information that the question asks for

Paragraph 3: write a finishing sentence

Read Abdul's letter to Jim.

1 Does it have good organisation?
2 Does it answer the question?
3 Are there any parts of his letter that you find confusing?

> Dear Jim
>
> Thank you for your letter. In this letter you are telling me that next month is your brother's birthday.
>
> 'Happy birthday' from me. He will be 14ᵗʰ next month so you can buy something special. I don't know if he like music or not, but will be surprise if you buy any CD. If your brother like futbooll you can buy for him a booll so he can enjoy playen with his friend on a free time.
>
> Teenage boys in my country like this surprises. I hope you will enjoy the party.
>
> Lots of love   Abdul

Now write your letter in about 100 words.

Read question 8 opposite.

Linking: It's good to try and join some of your ideas with linking words e.g. *so, when, but, because, suddenly.* This will help your writing to 'read' better.

Read this student's story. Underline all the linking words.

> It was a warm evening in the summer. I was on my way to Andy. He had asked me to call in. As I had plenty of time I was walking slowly. It became darker. Suddenly I heard a cry. Not far away on a bridge I recognised two persons who were fighting. When I looked carefully I could see two boys. Then one of them pushed the other down the bridge into the water and ran away. By the time I arrived at the river and saw that the boy in the water was unconscious. Without a second thought I sprung into the river. I could catch him and bring him out of the water. I started with first aid. At first I thought he was dead but then he started to move his arms and to breathe. He was alive!

This story got top marks – Band 5 – because of: confident and ambitious use of language, a wide range of structures and vocabulary, good use of linking devices, being well organised.

Now write your story in about 100 words.

Part 3

Write an answer to **one** of the questions (**7** or **8**) in this part.
Write your answer in about **100 words** on your answer sheet.
Mark the question number in the box at the top of your answer sheet.

Question 7

- This is part of a letter you receive from your penfriend.

> Help! It's my brother's 14th birthday next month and I can't think of a present to give him. What do teenage boys like getting as presents in your country?

- Now write a letter, answering your penfriend's question.
- Write your **letter** on your answer sheet.

Question 8

- Your English teacher has asked you to write a story.
- Your story must have this title:

A very unusual evening

- Write your **story** on your answer sheet.

Listening • PART 1

TIP

Two of the three pictures may show **some** correct information but only one picture will show all the correct information.

Read the questions in Part 1 and look at the suggestions/questions below *before* you listen to the recording. Remember, in the exam you won't have time to write, but this exercise focuses your attention on what's important.

Question 1

Name the three different presents.

Question 2

In picture A you can see Joe, his grandmother and his father. Who do you think the woman in picture B is? And picture C?

Question 3

Which one word is the most important in this question? Underline it.

Question 4

Which word in the question is the most important?

Question 5

Write the time (e.g. 3.15) over each picture. Which word in the question do you think is particularly important?

Question 6

Name the three types of TV programme in the pictures.

Question 7

Name the three types of transport in the pictures.

Now listen to the recording and choose the correct pictures.

Part 1

Questions 1–7

There are seven questions in this part.
For each question there are three pictures and a short recording.
Choose the correct picture and put a tick (✔) in the box below it.

Example: Where did the man leave his camera?

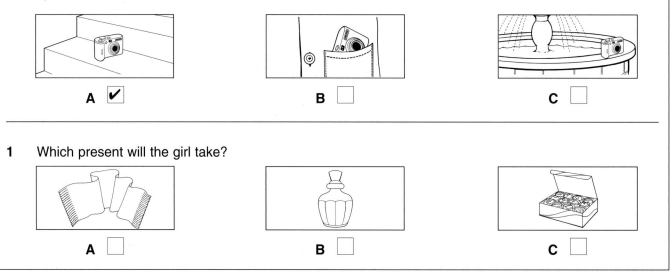

A ✔   B ☐   C ☐

---

1   Which present will the girl take?

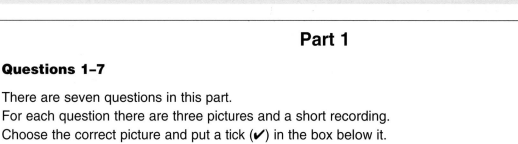

A ☐   B ☐   C ☐

2 Who lives in Joe's house now?

A  ☐ B  ☐ C ☐

3 Who will be on the stage next?

A  ☐ B  ☐ C ☐

4 Where is the woman's notebook now?

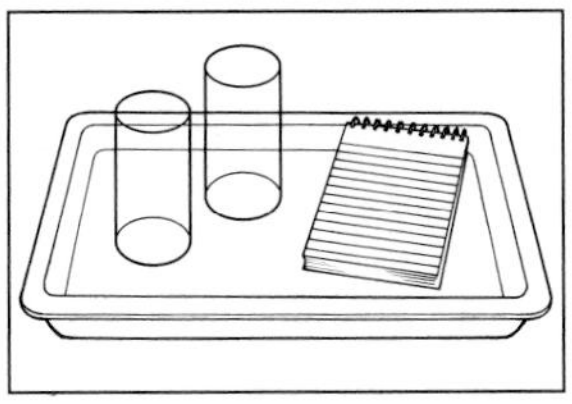

A 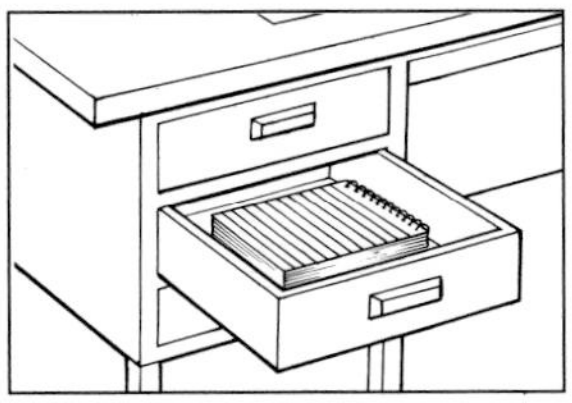 ☐ B  ☐ C ☐

5 What time will the cake be ready?

A  ☐ B  ☐ C ☐

6 Which TV programme will they watch together?

A  ☐ B  ☐ C ☐

7 How will the family get to Glasgow?

A  ☐ B  ☐ C ☐

TIP

The questions often use different words from the recording, for example, you hear: 'When I left school, I worked as a ...'
You read: 'Louise's first job was as a ...'

You will hear Louise Bright telling some students about her work as a clothes designer. Look at the questions below. Listen to the recording ONCE and answer these questions.

Question 8

Louise has had four different jobs. Can you put them in the order in which she did them?

sportswear designer ☐   secretary ☐

travel agent ☐   bank clerk ☐

Question 9

Louise did different things on her course at the London School of Fashion. Decide which she did in Year 1, Year 2 and Year 3.

Design and make clothes   Year ....

The history of fashion   Year ....

Work in a big store   Year ....

Question 10

Lots of people came to Louise's final fashion show, but who was she most pleased to have there?

Question 11

Does Louise say that the sports clothes are simple to make?   Yes/No

Why does Louise like the materials she uses for the sports clothes she makes?

Question 12

How many of Louise's fellow students are now working for famous fashion designers?

How many of Louise's fellow students are now working in advertising?

Question 13

Is earning a lot of money important to Louise?
     Yes/No

Now look at questions 8–13 opposite. Listen again to the recording and answer the questions.

Part 2

Questions 8–13

You will hear Louise Bright telling some students about her work as a clothes designer.
For each question, put a tick (✔) in the correct box.

---

8   Louise's first job was as a

A   bank clerk.   ☐

B   travel agent.   ☐

C   secretary.   ☐

9   In the first year of her course, Louise

A   learnt how to make clothes.   ☐

B   studied the history of fashion.   ☐

C   worked in a large clothes shop.   ☐

10   At the final fashion show, Louise says she was really pleased that

A   her parents saw her work.   ☐

B   all the college students worked well together.   ☐

C   owners of fashion businesses were there.   ☐

11   Louise says she really likes designing sports clothes because they are

A   produced in a variety of styles.   ☐

B   easy for her to make.   ☐

C   comfortable for people to wear.   ☐

12   Louise says that most students from her course now work

A   for well-known fashion designers.   ☐

B   for big stores.   ☐

C   in advertising.   ☐

13   Louise's aim is to

A   start a children's clothes business.   ☐

B   get to the top of her profession.   ☐

C   make a lot of money.   ☐

TIP

Check that what you've put in the gap makes sense. Make sure it 'fits' with what comes before and after it.

Read the instructions and questions about Finchbrooke Country Park below.

Think about the kind of information that will go in each gap.

Question 14

Will you be listening for a day or a time?

Question 15

Will you be listening for a number or a time?

Question 16

What could you get free from the Visitors' Centre?

Question 17

Can you think of a word for this gap? It has to be a noun (because of 'the') and it must fit with the words after the gap ('to the park').

Question 18

Look at the form of the words before and after the gap. You'll be listening for something similar. Any ideas?

Question 19

Can you think of anything that a group might have on a visit to the Country Park?

Now listen to the recording and fill in the missing information for questions 14–19.

Part 3

Questions 14–19

You will hear a recorded message about Finchbrooke Country Park.
For each question, fill in the missing information in the numbered space.

Finchbrooke Country Park

Opening times

Park:	Every day (8 a.m. – 7 p.m.)
Visitors' Centre:	**(14)** .... – Sunday (9 a.m. – 5.30 p.m.)

From the town centre, take bus number **(15)** ....

Inside the Visitors' Centre, you can buy books

and videos and get free **(16)** ....

If the Visitors' Centre is shut, a telephone can be found

at the **(17)** .... to the park.

In the park, you can go cycling, **(18)** .... and camping.

Group visits include a **(19)** .... and a guided tour.

TIP

Underline important words in the sentences (questions 20–25) to help you focus on what to listen for.

Read the instructions below, and look at sentences 20–25.

There some key words in each sentence. You need to underline them before you listen to the conversation.

Question 20: underline *both dislike*.

Question 21: underline the main verb and another piece of important information.

Continue with questions 22–25, underlining what you think you will need to listen carefully for.

Look at the sentences again. They contain some different verbs that express Tony and Rachel's feelings and opinions.

Think about what Tony and Rachel might actually say to express these opinions.

Now listen to the recording and decide if each sentence is correct or incorrect.

Part 4

Questions 20–25

Look at the six sentences for this part.
You will hear a conversation between a boy called Tony and a girl called Rachel, about watching television.
Decide if each sentence is correct or incorrect.
If it is correct, put a tick (✔) in the box under **A** for **YES**. If it is not correct, put a tick (✔) in the box under **B** for **NO**.

		A YES	B NO
20	Tony and Rachel both dislike watching cartoons.	☐	☐
21	Tony and Rachel both prefer watching television alone.	☐	☐
22	Rachel thinks her mother can afford to buy her a television.	☐	☐
23	Tony has kept his promise about watching television at night.	☐	☐
24	Rachel wants to be able to choose when she watches television.	☐	☐
25	Tony agrees with his parents' attitude towards homework.	☐	☐

Speaking • PART 1

TIP

During Part 1 of the Speaking Test, the interaction is between examiner and candidate, not candidate and candidate.

You may be asked questions about your hobbies or interests. Think what you could say about how you spend your time when you're not working or studying. How important are the following for you?

- music
- sport
- cinema & TV
- reading
- travel and visiting other places

Speaking • PART 2

TIP

Try and react to what your partner says. Think about what you do in your own language when you have a conversation, and do the same here.

Read what the examiner will say to you in Part 2 and look at the Picture Sheet on page 106 showing different ways the English friend can keep cool.

Imagine you and your partner are discussing the task. Think about how you can react to what your partner says.

Language box – agreeing and disagreeing

(That's) true. I agree. You're right. I think so too.

That's a good idea. / That's interesting.

Really? I'm not sure about that.
I don't think I agree because …
I don't think so because …
Yes, but …

Read part of the conversation between two students about this task. Do they use any of the language in the box above?

Student 1: So … I don't think it's a good idea if he eats ice-cream. I mean, it's nice but it only keeps you cool for a few minutes.

Student 2: You're right, but he might enjoy it. It's the same with a drink.

Student 1: I don't think so. Drinking is good for you when you're in a hot country. You should drink as much as possible.

Student 2: True. What about taking a shower? A cold one would be good in the morning and the evening.

Student 1: I think so too. I love showers when the weather is hot. It makes me feel fresh. So let's have a look at some of the other ideas.

If you're working with a partner, continue the conversation; make sure you both say more or less equal amounts.

Part 2 (2–3 minutes)

Interlocutor: *Say to both candidates:*
I'm going to describe a situation to you.
An English friend has to go to live in a very **hot** country for his work, but he doesn't **like** hot weather. Talk together about the different ways he can keep **cool** and then decide which will be **best**.
Here is a picture with some ideas to help you.
*Indicate the **Picture Sheet** on page 106 to the candidates.*
I'll say that again.
An English friend has to go to live in a very **hot** country for his work, but he doesn't **like** hot weather. Talk together about the different ways he can keep **cool** and then decide which will be **best**.
All right? Talk together.
Allow the candidates enough time to complete the task without intervention. Prompt only if necessary.
Thank you.

TIP

In Part 4, talk to each other. Don't talk to the examiner. Remember to ask each other questions as well as giving your own ideas.

PART 3

Read what the examiner will say to you in Part 3.

You have about one minute to talk about your photograph. A good description will include something about

- the people
- the action
- the place
- the background.

Read this description of photograph 5 on page 107. Look at how the different topics are included.

I can see a woman. She's wearing a blue shirt – I think she's a teacher – and she's sitting next to a boy. I don't know how old he is – maybe about 7 or 8. I think she's helping the boy to write. She looks kind. The boy has got a pencil in his hand. There are some books on the table and lots of pencils in a pot. I think they are in school because in the background I can see another child and a woman. Also there are some letters on the wall.

Practise doing the same with photograph 6 on page 107.

PART 4

Read what the examiner will say to you in Part 4.

Think about what you learn best from your family.

Think what you can add to these points, e.g.

I think I learnt how to behave from my family, because when I was a child my mother and my father always told me what was polite and what wasn't polite.

Think about what you learn best from your school – and say why.

If you're working with a partner, talk together about this task. Make sure you really do *talk to each other*.

Part 3 (3 minutes)

Interlocutor: *Say to both candidates:*
Now, I'd like each of you to talk on your own about something. I'm going to give each of you a photograph of people **looking** and **learning**.
Candidate A, here is your photograph. *(Indicate photograph 5 on page 107 to Candidate A.)* Please show it to Candidate B, but I'd like you, Candidate A, to talk about it. Candidate B, you just listen to Candidate A. I'll give you your photograph in a moment.
Candidate A, please tell us what you can see in your photograph.

Candidate A: *Approximately one minute.*
If there is a need to intervene, prompts rather than direct questions should be used.
Thank you.

Interlocutor: Now, Candidate B, here is your photograph. It also shows people **looking** and **learning**. *(Indicate photograph 6 on page 107 to Candidate B.)* Please show it to Candidate A and tell us what you can see in the photograph.

Candidate B: *Approximately one minute.*
Thank you.

Part 4 (3 minutes)

Interlocutor: *Say to both candidates:*
Your photographs showed people **looking** and **learning**. Now, I'd like you to talk together about the things which you learn best from your **family** and the things you learn best from your **school**.
Allow the candidates enough time to complete the task without intervention. Prompt only if necessary.
Thank you. That's the end of the test.

TEST 4

PAPER 1 ● Reading and Writing (1 hour 30 minutes)

Reading ● PART 1

TIP

When you transfer your answers to the answer sheet, make sure you check them and write them in the correct place.

Read the example text in Part 1 below and the answers to these questions:

a) How many films do you get? – Three
b) How many films do you pay for? – Two
c) Does it mention anything else about films or cameras? – No

So 'A' is the right answer because you get three films for the price of two. 'B' is wrong because it mentions buy one film and get one free. 'C' is wrong because it mentions *printing* films free, not the number of films.

Now answer these questions and choose the correct letter in Part 1.

1 a) Is the notice for lorry drivers or all drivers?
   b) Are lorries or cars turning into this road?
   c) Should drivers drive more slowly or leave the road?

2 a) What does Annie suggest buying for Mum?
   b) Does she say it is too expensive?
   c) Is Annie going to pay for the present by herself?

3 a) Does the notice say that there will be no trains?
   b) Does the notice say you will be going a different way?
   c) Will the trains be early or late? Why?

4 a) What did Andrea do yesterday?
   b) What two things did she do today?
   c) What did she do first today?

5 a) Are Kitchens Direct going to phone you?
   b) Are Kitchens Direct changing the quality of their products?
   c) Do Kitchens Direct ask you to speak to them if there is a problem?

Part 1

Questions 1–5

Look at the text in each question.
What does it say?
Mark the correct letter **A**, **B**, or **C** on your answer sheet.

Example:

0

REGENCY CAMERAS
Buy two films
and get one
FREE

A Buy three films for the price of two.

B Get a free film with every one you buy.

C Films bought here are printed free.

Answer:

0	A	B	C
	▬	☐	☐

1

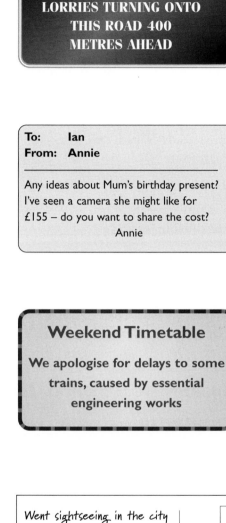

DRIVERS

REDUCE SPEED NOW LORRIES TURNING ONTO THIS ROAD 400 METRES AHEAD

A Lorry drivers should slow down within the next 400 metres.

B Drivers can avoid slow traffic by turning onto another road in 400 metres.

C Drive more slowly as lorries are joining the road 400 metres ahead.

2

To: Ian
From: Annie

Any ideas about Mum's birthday present? I've seen a camera she might like for £155 – do you want to share the cost?
            Annie

A Annie suggests that she and Ian give Mum one birthday pesent between hem.

B The present Annie saw for Mum was too expensive, so she needs other ideas.

C Annie has already bought Mum's present but has seen something Ian could buy.

3

Weekend Timetable

We apologise for delays to some trains, caused by essential engineering works

This weekend, some trains

A will be cancelled.

B will take a different route.

C will be late.

4

Went sightseeing in the city today after looking round the museum. Visited a wonderful castle on the way to the beach yesterday.
Back Friday.
            Andrea

A Andrea went sightseeing after she went to the beach yesterday.

B Andrea visited the museum before she went sightseeing.

C Andrea went to the beach before she visited a castle.

5

KITCHENS DIRECT

Tell us if our products ever fall below the quality you expect

A We will inform you if our kitchen products take longer to deliver than expected.

B We are continuing to improve the quality of our kitchen products.

C We need to know if there is something wrong with our kitchen products.

TIP

Be careful: the people in Part 2 often have three or four needs/interests. Some of the texts will only match with maybe two of these needs.

Read about the people below. <u>Underline</u> what the people want. Read each text opposite and <u>underline</u> what each campsite offers.

The questions have been answered wrongly.

Question 6: H

Karl and Matthias want four things. Campsite H only gives them two. What makes it unsuitable?
It doesn't offer any sunbathing and swimming and the town is lively – Karl and Matthias wanted to stay away from busy towns.

Question 7: E

Carlos and Ana want four things. What's the problem with the sport offered at campsite E?

Question 8: C

Mick and Jackie have three needs. Which one is missing from campsite C?

Question 9: A

Angela has three needs. Which two things are missing from campsite A?

Question 10: F

The Dupont family have three needs. Why is campsite F not suitable for them?

Now, choose the right answers for questions 6–10.

Part 2

Questions 6–10

The people below all want to spend their holidays camping in the UK.
On the opposite page there are descriptions of eight campsites.
Decide which campsite would be the most suitable for the following people.
For questions **6–10**, mark the correct letter (**A–H**) on your answer sheet.

---

6  Karl and Matthias are studying English at university. They want a cheap holiday, swimming and sunbathing, with some nightlife. They want to stay away from busy towns.

7  Carlos and Ana Alberola would like a relaxing holiday at a quiet campsite with beautiful scenery. They are both good swimmers, and want to learn other water sports. They don't want to cook for themselves every day.

8  Mick and Jackie are interested in visiting historic buildings. Their nine-year-old son Steven likes looking after animals and playing on the beach.

9 Angela enjoys walking in the countryside, and wants to try climbing in a group. As she will be in the open air all day, she needs to buy food to take with her.

10  The Dupont family want a seaside campsite where their children, aged five and eight, can join in organised activities, while the parents go walking in the countryside.

Campsites in the UK – Top Choices

A   Valley Camping
This campsite is in a peaceful location, within minutes of a safe, sandy beach, and an hour from a pretty market town. Inland, there are castles and churches to visit. Valley Camping has a swimming pool and supermarket on site.

B   Mountjoy Camping
Popular with couples and families with children, Mountjoy is a lively campsite all year round. The site leads straight onto the beach where a holiday club offers 5- to 10-year-olds plenty to do, leaving adults free to enjoy themselves. Mountjoy is surrounded by fields, away from busy towns and villages.

C   Seaview Camping
Seaview has beaches, caves and islands to explore a short distance away. There is a lake for fishing and children can feed the ducks. The swimming pool has exciting waterslides and under-5s can use the nursery pool. Seaview has an ice-cream café and juice bar on-site.

D   Lakeside
This luxury campsite offers something for everyone, and even has some fields for tents away from the main site which are less busy. There are countryside views, pony rides and a soccer camp for children. The lake offers canoe hire and water-skiing lessons, with a separate area for fishing. An evening bus service goes to the nearby town with its many bars and restaurants.

E   Connolly's Camping
Definitely an excellent holiday spot for the sporty, Connolly's offers a swimming pool, bike hire and mountain walks led by experienced guides. The area is a dream for nature lovers with forests and wildlife. A snack bar and a small supermarket are on-site. Dining facilities at several nearby hotels.

F   Parkside Holiday Village
This is a reasonably-priced campsite with superb, sandy beaches nearby. The main attraction is the pool with waterslides and waves. Along with evening entertainment, there are nightly discos in a hotel near the campsite. Inland, there are quiet villages for sightseeing.

G   Freshwater Bay
This newly-opened campsite is located next to clean beaches with caves and rock pools to explore. Sunbathers can hire chairs for a small charge. Attractions include ancient castles, churches and pretty fishing villages. The campsite farm welcomes visitors, who can help with the cows, chickens and sheep. Fresh farm food is also on sale here.

H   The Two Fountains
This is an inexpensive riverside campsite, a short walk from a busy ferry port. The town is lively during the day with pavement cafés and souvenir shops. However, there are few cultural attractions and little choice of evening entertainment.

TIP

You may meet some unfamiliar vocabulary when you read the text. Don't worry because you will not need to understand this in order to answer a question correctly. Concentrate on finding the specific information from the text.

First, read sentences 11–20 about collecting postcards.

<u>Underline</u> the information in the sentences that you will need to look for in the text, e.g.
Sentence 11: … <u>more popular than collecting stamps</u> …

Read the text for the information you need and <u>underline</u> it. Do this question by question.

If you have difficulty deciding if a sentence is correct or incorrect, turn the sentence into a question, e.g.

Sentence 11: *Is collecting postcards more popular than collecting stamps?*

Part 3

Questions 11–20

Look at the sentences below about collecting postcards.
Read the text on the opposite page to decide if each sentence is correct or incorrect.
If it is correct, mark **A** on your answer sheet.
If it is not correct, mark **B** on your answer sheet.

---

11   Collecting postcards is generally believed to be more popular than collecting stamps.

12   Visitors will be able to buy postcards from 120 different traders at the Picture Postcard Show.

13   Harry Taylor has helped to run the Picture Postcard Show for ten years.

14   People choose to collect postcards partly because they are affordable.

15   Collectors expect to pay a maximum of £30 for an unusual postcard.

16   Collectors are particularly interested in postcards that were printed between 1900 and 1918.

17   It was possible to receive mail seven times a day in London between 1900 and 1918.

18   Before 1902, the Post Office only accepted postcards with senders' messages written next to the picture.

19   Postcards of popular seaside towns that were printed in the early 1900s are valuable.

20   A card without a message is worth more than the same card with writing on it.

Collecting Picture Postcards

It is thought to be second only to stamp collecting as a collector's interest, and each year in August the biggest show of its kind worldwide takes place in London. Collecting postcards is a growing market, with fans all around the world, thousands of whom will be in England for this year's Picture Postcard Show. There will be exhibitions of a wide range of postcards and many will be on sale from the 120 UK and international traders who will also be there.

'Postcard collecting is growing very fast,' says Harry Taylor, who collects postcards of ships and, as chairman of the Postcard Traders' Association, has been one of the organisers of the London show for the last ten years. The price is one of the reasons why collectors are attracted to postcards. Although the special cards cost more, you can spend anything between 5p and £30 for the typical cards on the market. 'This means you can put a wonderful collection together for very little,' he says.

Sports, transport, buildings and animals are the most popular, but there are other less well-known subjects as well. One American collector recently started a website showing his collection of postcards on the early history of cotton. The site has already had more than 1,000 visitors.

Postcards that appeared between 1900 and 1918 are the ones that attract the most attention. 'At that time, the cost of sending a letter or postcard was less than a penny. They emptied the boxes every hour in London and the post would sometimes be delivered seven times a day,' says Paul Marshall, who works at Asquith's Auctioneers, which holds three postcard sales a year. Picture postcards, as opposed to blank cards, came to Britain from other European countries, but it was not until the 1890s that they were accepted by the Post Office. In 1902, Mr Marshall says, the rules were changed again, allowing both message and address to be put on the same side. Before that, the message had to be written beside the picture.

Just because a postcard is old it does not mean it is valuable. For example, seaside views produced in large quantities at the beginning of the last century are not likely to be worth very much. Whatever the subject of the postcard, the condition is very important. The value of the postcard also increases if there is a message, which then gives it more social or historical value.

TIP

Read the text once and make sure you understand the topic and general meaning. Read it a second time, but more carefully.

Read the text below.

Questions after first reading:

1 Who is the writer?
2 What is he writing about?
3 Who did he talk to?
4 What did the swimmers feel about their activity?
5 Did the writer enjoy being in the water?

Now, read the text again.

Read the questions below and see if you can write your own answers. Don't look at the A/B/C/D choices opposite.

Question 21

What is the writer trying to do in this text?

Question 22

What can a reader find out from this text?

Question 23

What does Peter Smith say about his morning swim?

Question 24

What did the writer feel about swimming at the pool?

Question 25

What do you think the writer would say about the experience to his friends?

Some of what you wrote above may be in the A/B/C/D choices opposite. Look at these now, and choose the right answer.

Part 4

Questions 21–25

Read the text and questions below.
For each question, mark the correct letter **A**, **B**, **C** or **D** on your answer sheet.

Breaking the Ice

Michael Sharp visits an outdoor pool

It's just before 7 a.m. and I'm at an outdoor swimming pool in London, where the temperature of the water is only 11 degrees above freezing! Amazingly, there are already eight people swimming.

I had intended to discover, by taking a swim myself, why anyone would want to swim in such cold water. However, in the end, I decided to ask people instead. Peter Smith has been a swimmer here for three years, coming every morning before work. 'It's wonderful on a cold winter morning,' he says. 'I thought it would make me healthier and I haven't been ill once since I started.'

All the swimmers here say the same thing. They all feel fitter. However, not everyone agrees with them. Some doctors say it helps fight illness, while others say it could be dangerous, especially for your heart.

I asked Peter what they did on the days when the pool was frozen. 'That's easy,' he said. 'There's a place in the middle where the ice is thin and easy to break. You have to avoid the sides where the ice is thicker. I did try to swim there once just to see what it was like, but I found that it was impossible to break through the ice.'

I would like to be able to say that I too dived happily into the water and swam a couple of hundred metres. But the truth is, fearing the worst, I walked very carefully into the pool, stood there almost in shock and then got out again after 30 seconds before I became a block of ice!

21 What is the writer trying to do in this text?

  A explain why some people like swimming in the cold

  B prove an idea he has had about keeping fit

  C warn people not to go swimming in cold water

  D advise people on ways to stay healthy

22 What can a reader find out from this text?

  A where to go swimming in London

  B what happened to the writer at the pool

  C how to keep warm in cold water

  D how often the writer goes swimming

23 What does Peter Smith say about his morning swim?

  A It has helped him recover from a recent illness.

  B He enjoys it when the pool is covered in ice.

  C It is the reason why he keeps well all year.

  D He thinks it makes him work better.

24 What did the writer feel about swimming at the pool?

  A It was as cold as he expected.

  B He did not like the ice.

  C It made him feel healthier.

  D He enjoyed swimming up and down.

25 What do you think the writer would say to his friends?

  A

  My doctor has advised me not to go swimming there.

  B

  It's amazing how the pool stays clear of ice all winter.

  C

  I really enjoyed my early morning swim at the outdoor pool.

  D

  I was surprised at the number of people in the pool – they must be crazy.

TIP

When you read the text for the second time, think about a possible word for the gap before you look at the choices.

Read the title. Write in the example answer in space (0). Read the text without looking at the choices.

Someone has answered the questions, but they have made some mistakes. **Two of the answers are correct, but eight are wrong.** Look carefully at all the gaps, and ask yourself questions:

- Does the word make sense?
- Does it fit grammatically?
- Are there any words after the gap that are important?

Correct the wrong answers.

Part 5

Questions 26–35

Read the text below and choose the correct word for each space.
For each question, mark the correct letter **A**, **B**, **C** or **D** on your answer sheet.

Example:

| 0 | **A** worked | **B** earned | **C** operated | **D** employed |

Answer:

0	A	B	C	D

Jacqui Swift

Jacqui Swift has **(0)** .... as a journalist for newspapers, a music magazine and TV programmes. At the **(26)** .... , she is writing for a music website **(27)** .... started last month.

'I **(28)** .... to write for the internet because this is where you find the very latest information about bands. I love the speed of the internet. I can write a piece in the morning and see it **(29)** .... on the website in the afternoon. The same story won't be in the newspapers **(30)** .... the next day. It may **(31)** .... up to six weeks before you see it in some magazines.

I am a **(32)** .... of a team. We have to work fast and mustn't make any **(33)** .... , so it can be stressful. But we all get along **(34)** .... with each other. I find it really exciting to think that our work **(35)** .... read all round the world!'

26 **A** period **(B)** time **C** moment **D** date

27 **(A)** which **B** what **C** who **D** when

28 **(A)** thought **B** persuaded **C** imagined **D** decided

29 **A** show **(B)** appear **C** attend **D** display

30 **(A)** over **B** during **C** towards **D** until

31 **A** take **(B)** last **C** stay **D** remain

32 **A** worker **B** colleague **C** member **(D)** person

33 **(A)** faults **B** mistakes **C** accidents **D** failures

34 **(A)** good **B** strongly **C** well **D** happy

35 **A** is **B** will **(C)** has **D** does

TIP

Be careful when you complete the sentence. Read the whole sentence to check that your words fit.

Look at questions 1–5 below. The sentences have been completed, but they are all wrong. Complete the sentences correctly:

1 Martina asked me 'Would you .... join my band?'

2 Martina's band has played in concerts .... two years.

3 Her old band was not .... as her new one.

4 There .... in Martina's band.

5 You don't .... pay anything to get into their concerts.

Part 1

Questions 1–5

Here are some sentences about playing in a band.
For each question, complete the second sentence so that it means the same as the first.
Use no more than three words.
Write only the missing words on your answer sheet.
You may use this page for any rough work.

Example:

0   Last year, I was given a guitar by my father.

Last year, my father .... **a guitar.**   ***Answer:*** | 0 | *gave me* |

---

1   My friend Martina asked me if I wanted to join her band.

Martina asked me 'Would you *want*... **join my band?'**

2   Martina's band started playing concerts two years ago.

Martina's band has played in concerts *since*... **two years.**

3   Her new band is better than her old one.

Her old band was not *better*... **as her new one.**

4   Martina's band has six people in it.

There *six people*..................................... **in Martina's band.**

5   The tickets for their concerts are free.

You don't *need*... **pay anything to get into their concerts.**

TIP

Use informal language for your messages and emails. Imagine you're talking to someone.

First, read question 6 below.

Make sure you understand what the situation is:

1 Who's going to the cinema?
2 When?
3 Why are you leaving a note for Dan?

Make notes on the following three points that you have to include:

- which cinema you're going to
- what film you plan to see
- what time you will meet Dan

Write your note in 35–45 words.

Read these students' answers.

1

Hi Dan

Tonight my friends and I are going to see a film in Sestri's cinema. Would you like to come? The film is very interesting: two tourists got lost into a wood and they must find the way to go out, but in the wood there is something else...
The film isn't for frightening people! If you decide to come, we'll meet at the bar near the cinema at 2.30p.m.
We are waiting for you!
    Monika

2

Hello Dan,
I decided to go to the cinema Old Town.
We would like to see film 'With out word'.
I will meet you outside cinema at 6.15pm. on Saturday see you here.
    Boro

a) Do they both include all three points?   Yes/No
b) Is any information wrong in either note?   Yes/No

Make some changes so that notes 1 and 2 are better.

Part 2

Question 6

Dan, an American student who is staying with you, wants to go to the cinema tonight with you and your friends.

Write a note to leave for Dan. In your note, you should

- tell Dan which cinema you are going to
- say what film you plan to see
- suggest what time you will meet Dan.

Write **35–45 words** on your answer sheet.

Read question 7 opposite.

Read this student's answer.

Hello, Dear Sandra
I receved your letter last Monday I hope you well I think is the best for you visited a city, because in a city there a lots of place Interesting, museums, lake, sHops, Markets, and, churchs I think so you like it, and on the evening you can go out eating in an good restaurants, and dancin in an funny place, I think it very better the last week Holiday, we going to visiting countryside for 2 days, it's very quite and there are a beatiful scenery, we can walking in the mauntain.

This letter was marked Band 2 and described by the examiner as an 'inadequate attempt'. There are many mistakes and a lot of effort is needed from the reader. Correct the letter, paying particular attention to these basic mistakes:

- punctuation – no full stops, and wrong use of capital letters
- organisation – no paragraphs, no signature
- grammar – problems with singulars and plurals e.g. a lots of
- spelling – six mistakes

Look at the question again. Write a 100-word letter using your own ideas.

Read question 8 opposite.

Before you write, think about:
- the verb tenses you will use
- who the email was from
- what it said
- if it was a good or bad surprise
- what you did
- what the result was

Now write a 100-word story beginning *'I was really surprised when I read the email.'*

TIP

You're asked to use about 100 words in your answer. If you write less than 80 words you cannot get maximum marks; longer answers are not automatically given a lower mark, but they may contain information that is not relevant to the question.

Part 3

Write an answer to one of the questions (**7** or **8**) in this part.
Write your answer in about **100 words** on your answer sheet.
Mark the question number in the box at the top of your answer sheet.

Question 7

- This is part of a letter you receive from some English friends.

For our next holiday, we want to visit your country.

Is it best to spend our time in a city or in the countryside?

Which would you recommend and why?

- Write a letter, answering your friends' questions.
- Write your **letter** on your answer sheet.

Question 8

- Your English teacher has asked you to write a story.
- Your story must begin with this sentence.

I was really surprised when I read the email.

- Write your **story** on your answer sheet.

Listening ● PART 1

> **TIP**
>
> It's not a good idea to change your answers when you are transferring them to the answer sheet.

Read questions 1–7 below and opposite and look at the pictures. <u>Underline</u> any important words in the questions.

Think about some vocabulary which you think you'll hear on the recording, e.g.

Question 1: *earrings, watch, pen*

Listen to the recording and answer the questions. Remember you will hear each recording twice.

Part 1

Questions 1–7

There are seven questions in this part.
For each question there are three pictures and a short recording.
Choose the correct picture and put a tick (✔) in the box below it.

Example: How did the woman get to work?

A ✔   B ☐   C ☐

---

1   Which present has the girl bought her mother?

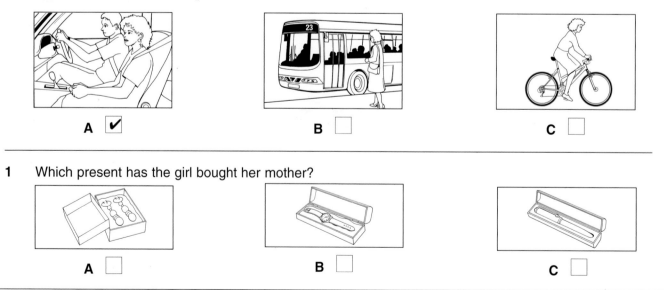

A ☐   B ☐   C ☐

2 What will the prize be in the painting competition?

A  ☐   B 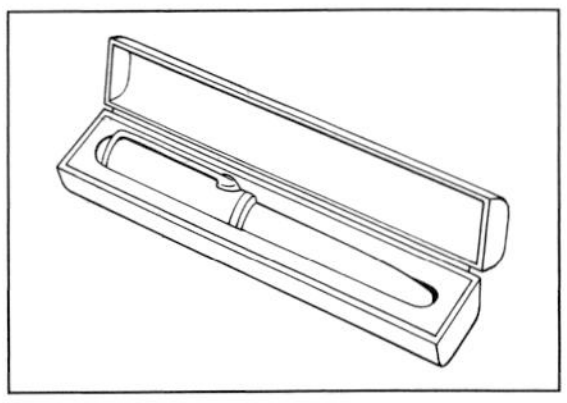 ☐   C ☐

3 Which photo does the girl dislike?

A  ☐   B  ☐   C ☐

4 What should the students take on the school trip?

A  ☐   B  ☐   C ☐

5 Which subject does the boy like best?

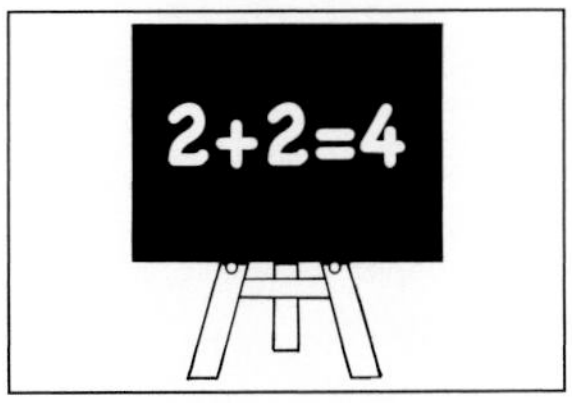

2+2=4

A 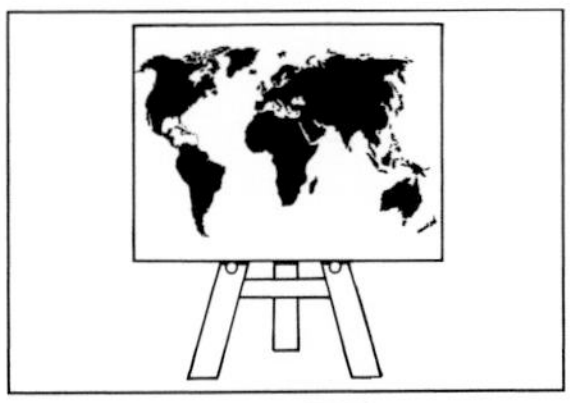 ☐   B  ☐   C ☐

6 What time is the dance class today?

A  ☐   B  ☐   C ☐

7 Which vegetables do they decide to put in the curry?

A  ☐   B 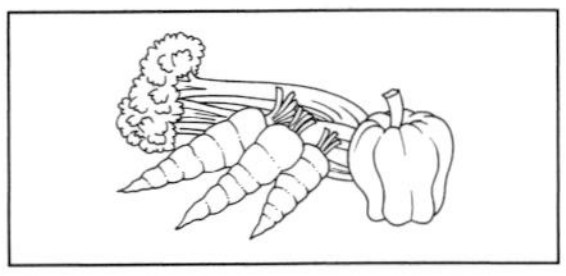 ☐   C ☐

TIP

If you have problems answering any of the questions, think about how you would answer it in your own words. Then look at the A/B/C choices again.

You're going to hear a man talking to a group of people about the band he plays in. Don't look at the questions opposite yet.

First, listen to the recording and write your own answers to questions 8–13.

Question 8

The music that the band plays is …

Question 9

The members of the band …

(This is a difficult question to complete because it's very open. Think about what all the members of the band have in common.)

Question 10

The band will only play your favourite song if …

Question 11

How many people are there in the band?

Question 12

Why was Bob chosen to join the band?

Question 13

Where does the band perform *most regularly*?

Now look at the A/B/C choices for questions 8–13 opposite.

Listen again, and choose the correct answer.

Part 2

Questions 8–13

You will hear a man talking to a group of people about the band he plays in.
For each question, put a tick (✔) in the correct box.

8   The music that the band plays is

    A easy for people to dance to. ☐

    B intended for young people. ☐

    C nice to hear while you're eating. ☐

9   The members of the band

    A all do similar jobs. ☐

    B have all studied music. ☐

    C all play music for pleasure. ☐

10   The band will only play your favourite song if

    A you ask them before the party. ☐

    B you give them the music. ☐

    C it is from the 1970s. ☐

11   How many people are there in the band?

    A six ☐

    B eight ☐

    C twelve ☐

12   Why was Bob chosen to join the band?

    A He was good at playing guitar. ☐

    B They were looking for a singer. ☐

    C They heard him singing somewhere. ☐

13   Where does the band perform most regularly?

    A in a hotel ☐

    B on a boat ☐

    C at weddings ☐

TIP

Listen carefully. If the answer is a date (for example question 14 below), you will probably hear two or more dates on the recording. Make sure you choose the one that is correct for the question.

The answers have already been filled in. All these words are mentioned on the recording but unfortunately they are <u>not</u> the right answers.

Listen to the recording and correct the information.

Read the instructions and questions about climbing holidays in North Wales.

Part 3

Questions 14–19

You will hear part of a radio programme about climbing holidays in North Wales.
For each question, fill in the missing information in the numbered space.

Climbing in North Wales

- The Climbing Centre first opened in **(14)** ....1869.............

- Climbing courses are held from March until **(15)** ....November.........

- Accommodation for a maximum of 70 people

The Four-day Course

Costs £280. Includes everything except **(16)** ....equipment.........

Day One

How to use a **(17)** ....route.................

Day Two

Understanding the weather

Days Three and Four

Two-day trip with one night in a **(18)** ....camping.........

Evening activities in the Centre

TV or **(19)** ....restaurants.......

TIP

Be careful when you transfer your answers to the answer sheet. And remember to put a ✔ in the correct box, not a ✗.

Read the instructions and sentences 20–25 below.

<u>Underline</u> the main verbs in each sentence, and any other pieces of information that you will have to listen carefully for.

Look carefully at the <u>underlined</u> verbs in sentences 21, 23, 24 and 25. Think about how these might be expressed in the conversation.

Listen to the conversation between Jack and Sarah about learning to drive.

Answer as many of the questions as possible. If you have difficulty deciding whether a sentence is correct or incorrect, turn it into a question. It's sometimes easier to work with questions rather than statements, e.g. Question 20: *Does Jack think his driving teacher's instructions are clear?*

Listen to the conversation again and check your answers.

Part 4

Questions 20–25

Look at the six sentences for this part.
You will hear a conversation between a boy, Jack, and a girl, Sarah, about learning to drive.
Decide if each sentence is correct or incorrect.
If it is correct, put a tick (✔) in the box under **A** for **YES**. If it is not correct, put a tick (✔) in the box under **B** for **NO**.

		A YES	B NO
20	Jack thinks that his driving teacher's instructions are clear.	☐	☐
21	Sarah <u>agrees</u> that learning to brake quickly is difficult.	☐	☐
22	Jack thinks he will be nervous on the day of the test.	☐	☐
23	Sarah <u>feels sure</u> that Jack will pass his driving test.	☐	☐
24	Sarah <u>allows</u> other people to drive her car.	☐	☐
25	Jack <u>intends</u> to save his money to buy his own car.	☐	☐

Speaking ● PART 1

TIP

In this part of the Speaking Test, don't interrupt when your partner is speaking.

In this part of the test, you may be asked questions about your study and your plans.

Think what you would say about:
- what you're studying or where you're working at the moment
- what languages you speak, and what you will do with English in the future
- what you would like to do in the future – for study, for work, etc.

Speaking ● PART 2

TIP

You only have about two or three minutes for this part of the test. You and your partner(s) should try and say something about all of the ideas on the picture sheet.

Read what the examiner will say to you in Part 2 and look at the ideas for the different kinds of museums on the Picture Sheet on page 108.

At the end of this part, you and your partner(s) might want to talk about which museum will be the most interesting. Look at the language below:

Language box – ending the discussion

What have we decided?
What do you think we should choose?
Shall we choose one?
Let's choose / go for …
OK, we've decided.
So, we think he/they should …

Read the final part of the conversation between three students about this task. Do they use any of the language from the box above?

Student 1: So, we've talked about all the different museums. Which will be the most interesting? What do you think we should choose?

Student 2: Well, I think they should go to the space museum because it's modern and they can do lots of things there.

Student 3: I don't think many people are interested in space. For me the animals look the most interesting.

Student 1: I'd like that one, but the other one that looks nice is the history of clothes.

Student 2: Well, let's go for the animal one. You both think that's good and I'm happy with that too.

Students 2 & 3: OK.

If you're working with a partner or partners, do this task from the beginning.

Part 2 (2–3 minutes)
Suitable for groups of three and pairs

Interlocutor: *Say to both / all candidates:*
I'm going to describe a situation to you.
A group of friends is visiting a **large city**.
They want to choose a **museum** to go to.
Talk together about the different **types** of museum they can visit and say which will be the most **interesting**.
Here is a picture with some ideas to help you.
*Indicate **Picture Sheet** on page 108 to the candidates. **N.B.** One A3 sheet to be shared.*
I'll say that again.
A group of friends is visiting a **large city**. They want to choose a **museum** to go to.
Talk together about the different **types** of museum they can visit and say which will be the most **interesting**.
All right? Talk together.
Allow the candidates enough time to complete the task without intervention. Prompt only if necessary.
Thank you.

TIP

If you're working in a group of three, make sure all of you have the chance to speak in Part 4.

PART 3

Read what the examiner will say to you in Part 3.

Read this description of photograph 7 on page 109:

'I can see a man who's working on his laptop with his left hand and he's eating something at the same time. He looks a bit worried. I think he could be at work, or maybe he's taken his laptop to a restaurant, and he's eating lunch. He's wearing a white suit and a red tie, and in the background I can see some other people who are also eating lunch. I think it's a self-service restaurant at their office. He is the only person with a computer, so maybe he's late with some work. I don't think it's very good for him to eat and work at the same time. He should relax during his lunch break.'

Check that this description includes something about:

- the people
- the action
- the place
- the background.

Use photographs 8 and 9 to practise doing a similar-style description. Time yourself. See what one minute feels like.

PART 4

Read what the examiner will say to you in Part 4.

You are asked to talk about when you use computers, and how you will use computers in the future.

'I use my computer for my studies. I have one at home and there are also ones we can use at school. I don't use them in lessons, but I use them if I want to write an essay, or if I want to find something out on the internet. And of course I use them for homework and for making things look good. My handwriting is terrible so computers are really good for me. What about you? When do you use computers?'

Continue the conversation. Then talk about how you will use computers in the future.

Part 3 (3 minutes)

Interlocutor: *Say to both / all candidates:*
Now, I'd like each of you to talk on your own about something. I'm going to give each of you a photograph of someone using a **computer**.
Candidate A, here is your photograph. *(Indicate photograph 7 on page 109 to Candidate A.)* Please show it to Candidates B and C, but I'd like you to talk about it. Candidates B and C, you just listen, I'll give you your photographs in a moment.
Candidate A, please tell us what you can see in your photograph.

Candidate A: *Approximately one minute.*
If there is a need to intervene, prompts rather than direct questions should be used.
Thank you.

Interlocutor: Now, Candidate B, here is your photograph. It also shows someone using a **computer**. *(Indicate photograph 8 on page 109 to Candidate B.)* Please show it to Candidates A and C and tell us what you can see in the photograph.

Candidate B: *Approximately one minute.*
Thank you.

Interlocutor: Now, Candidate C, here is your photograph. It also shows someone using a **computer**. *(Indicate photograph 9 on page 109 to Candidate C.)* Please show it to Candidates A and B and tell us what you can see in the photograph.

Candidate C: *Approximately one minute.*
Thank you.

Part 4 (3 minutes)

Interlocutor: *Say to both / all candidates:*
Your photographs showed people using **computers**. Now, I'd like you to talk together about times when **you** use computers and say what you think you will use them for in the **future**.
Allow the candidates enough time to complete the task without intervention. Prompt only if necessary.
Thank you. That's the end of the test.

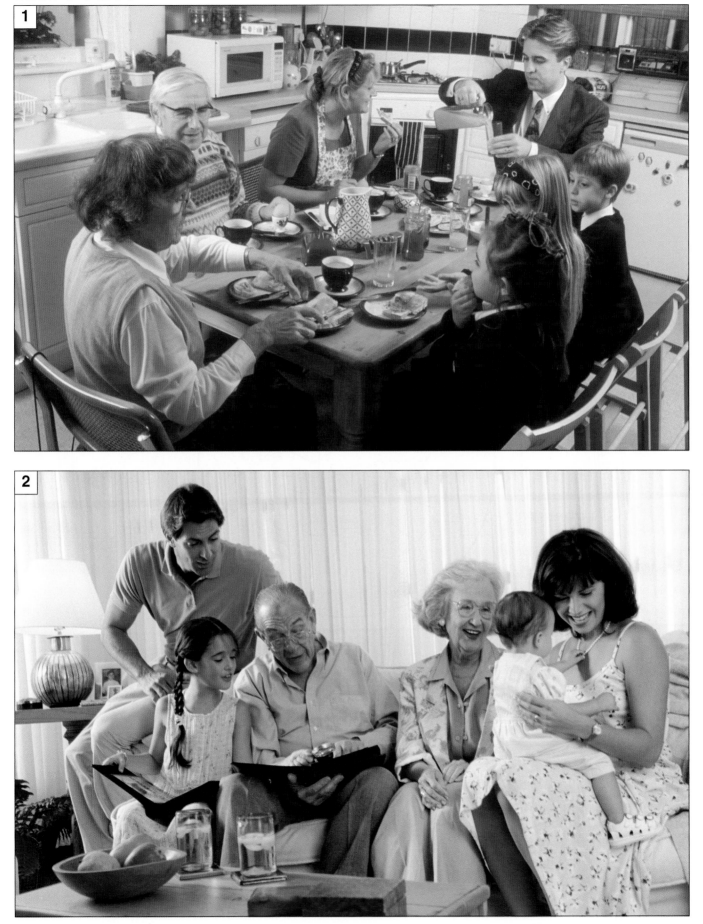

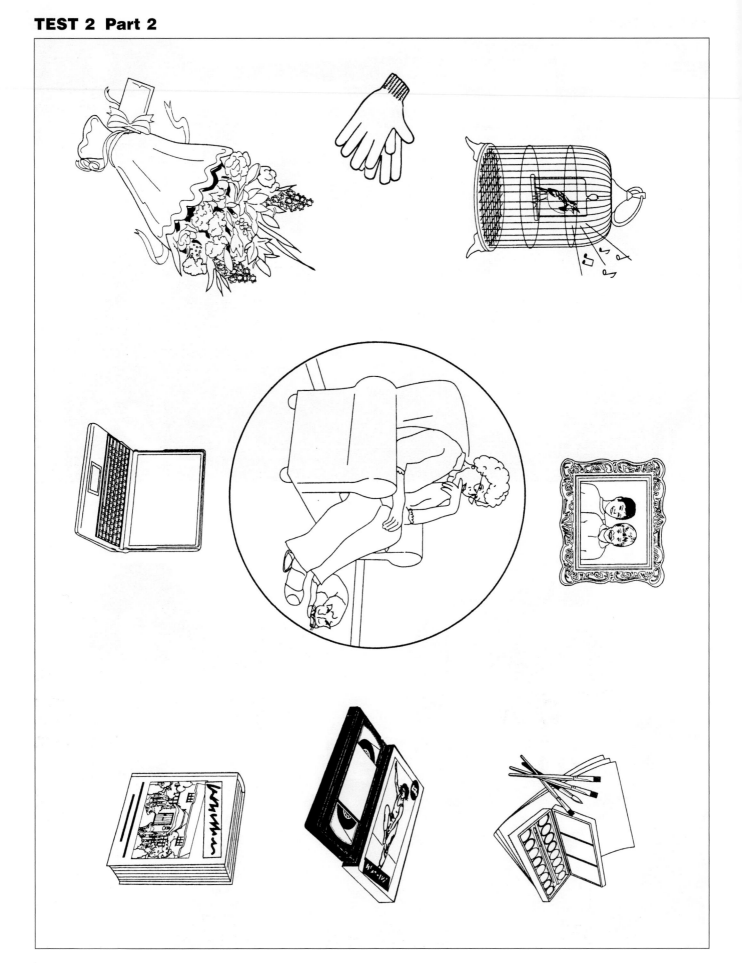

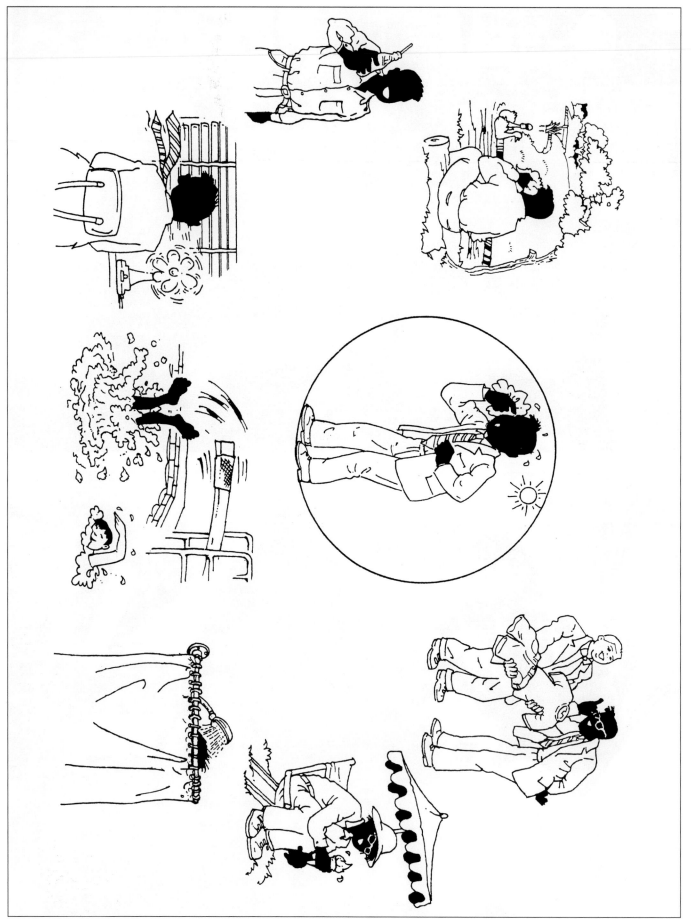

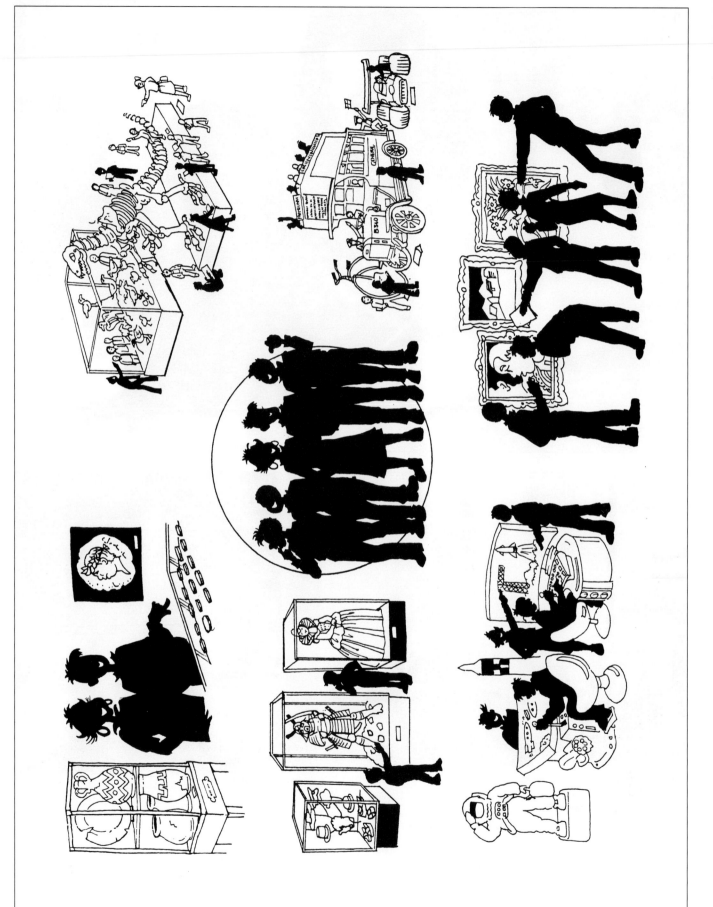

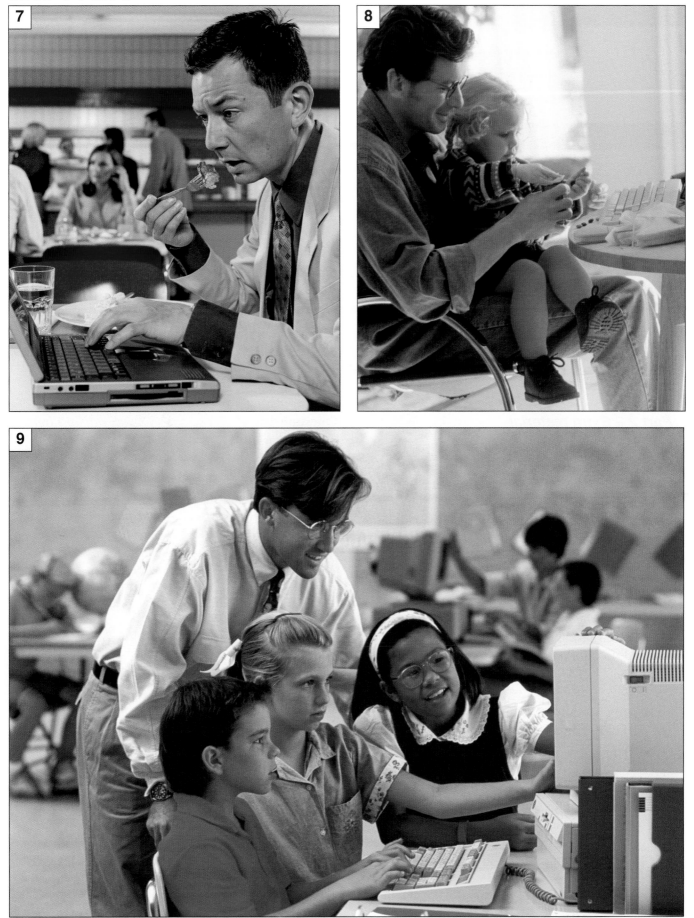

KEY

TEST 1

Reading

Part 1 – Extra material

Question 1: 1 A   2 A   3 take them
Question 2: 1 A   2 B   3 more than
Question 3: 1 B   2 B   3 after
Question 4: 1 B   2 B   3 A
Question 5: 1 A   2 B   3 break … careful

Part 1 – Exam material

1 C   2 B   3 C   4 A   5 A

Part 2 – Extra material

Question 7: lunch in a café; go surfing; relax in the sun
Question 8: relax on the beach; do some sport; buy some presents
Question 9: want to swim; go for a walk; children's play area; buy souvenirs
Question 10: lots of space; sit and enjoy the view; not manage difficult walk to the beach; eat lunch in a café

1 Because the nearest car park is 2 kms away. (also no possibility of learning to sail for no. 6 and no information about a café for no. 10)
2 no café
3 9
4 no opportunity to learn to sail
5 surfing is not permitted
6 10
7 swimming is dangerous; no car park
8 7
9 no information about learning to sail; no information about car parks
10 yes
11 It matches the people in question 6.

Part 2 – Exam material

6 H   7 D   8 F   9 A   10 C

Part 3 – Extra material

Question 12: ✔ text says: *have never made a film in your life, it doesn't matter.*
Question 13: ✔ text says: *the briefer the films, the more we can show.*
Question 14: ✘ text says: *you need to supply your own equipment*
Question 15: ✔ text says: *why not try writing your own music?*
Question 16: ✔ text says: *they watch each one from start to finish*
Question 17: ✔ text says: *you have to be less than 21 years old; if you are thinking about trying again in twelve months' time*
Question 18: ✘ text says: *if your film is chosen*
Question 19: ✔ text says: *if your film is chosen … you will get free entry to the festival*
Question 20: ✘ text says: *the competition closing date is Monday 11 May*

Part 3 – Exam material

11 B   12 A   13 A   14 B   15 A   16 A   17 A
18 B   19 A   20 B

Part 4 – Extra material

1 a leisure centre
2 a sports club
3 a local action group
4 sports facilities
5 less healthy activities; parking problems; problems for people living in area
6 yes; local hotel owners
7 a local newspaper reporter
8 no
Questions 21–25: students' own answers

Part 4 – Exam material

21 C 22 D 23 A 24 B 25 B

Part 5 – Extra material

1 He was a sailor, an explorer.
2 He made sure that they ate fresh fruit.
3 Tahiti, New Zealand, eastern Australia, Antarctica, islands of Pacific, Hawaii.

a prepositional phrase – on board
a pronoun – it
a quantity adjective – many
a 'time' word – during

Part 5 – Exam material

26 C 27 B 28 C 29 B 30 D 31 C
32 A 33 D 34 D 35 B

Writing

Part 1 – Extra material

1 b	2 <u>driving</u>
3 a	4 b
5 c	6 a
7 b	

Part 1 – Exam material

1 (was) opened 2 to drive 3 in / inside
4 because 5 until

Part 2 – Extra material

Ibrahima's email: I'm sorry; I have to go to see my grandfather; would you want to go dancing …
Jane's email: I'm very ill. I have got a flu.

Part 2 – Exam material

Task-specific Mark Scheme

- apology for **not being able to go**
- explanation of **why you can't go**
- suggestion of **something they can do the following weekend**

See page 26 for two candidate answers to this question.
Ibrahima's answer received a Band 5.
Jane's answer a Band 2.

Part 3 – Extra material

students' own answers

Part 3 – Exam material

Question 7: letter to a friend
Sample Answer A

> Dear Jane,
> thank you for your letter. I'm very surprised you've bought a video recorder. As I know you've always prefered going to the cinema to sitting at home in front of a TV, haven't you? Don't be angry with me, it's only a joke. You asked me to recommend you some good videos. Recently I've seen some, but the best of them is "Microcosmos". It's the right film for you - about the nature. But the authors show us round the nature in unusual way - you can see the life of the smallest animals, e.g. ants, snails, worms etc. It's amazing! And the music is wonderful. Try it and write me back. I'm looking forward to your opinion.
>   Love M

Examiner's comments

This is a very good attempt with confident and natural language, for example *you've always prefered going to the cinema to sitting at home in front of a TV, haven't you?* There is a wide range of structures and vocabulary, and it is well organised and linked. The errors are minor and non-impeding.

Band: 5

Sample Answer B

> Dear Olga,
> My best video I have seen recently is probably story for the whole family - especially for children - "The secret garden". It's romantic story from the beginnig of 20 century - . Everything in that film is nice and romantic - there is very nice nature, an old noble bilding, ugly persons and good ones. The best is the end - where as in every fairy tail the good wins. I like music, actors - just everything. I can suggest you this film for your children.
>   Jana

Examiner's comments

This is a good attempt with some ambitious language, for example *The best is the end – where as in every fairy tail the good wins.* There is evidence of organisation and a more than adequate range of structures and vocabulary. However a number of non-impeding errors, for example *It's romantic story from the beginning of 20 century* keep it out of Band 5.

Band: 4

Question 8: I woke up knowing …
Sample Answer C

I woke up knowing it was the most important day of my life. That time I was six and from last night I was worry. I can say I had two feeling, bad and good, happy and unhappy. My parents tried to help me and they said don't worry, It isn't dangerous. You can go and come back. We are sure you will enjoy. But I cried and cried. From one week ago we went shopping and they bought clothes and other things for me. Every day I tried to open capboard and I watch new clothes and new shoes. But they have told me that I can not use it until Saturday. Anyway on Saturday I started to go to school and I became a student and it was a start for learning.

Examiner's comments

This adequate attempt shows evidence of ambition but the language is flawed, for example *That time I was six and from last night I was worry.* There is an adequate range of structures and vocabulary, but also a number of mostly non-impeding errors, for example *Every day I tried to open capboard and I watch new clothes and new shoes.* Some effort is required from the reader, especially to sort out the tense sequence.

Band: 3

Sample Answer D

I woke up knowing it was the most important day of my life. Because I had a interview in the university of London on that day. My friend Jin Ce and I had just finished our foundation course study. IN these few monthes, we were busy in finding university. I'd chose lots of university, in the end we decided to go to London.
We went to London by train. When we got there, we saw lots of students was waiting for the interview …
Luckly, we got it. After the summer, both of us can study at University of London. That's really great.
We are very happy and we will study hard very much.

Examiner's comments

In this attempt the range of structures and vocabulary is adequate, for example *My friend Jin Ce and I had just finished our foundation course study.* There is evidence of organisation and some linking of sentences, for example *When we got there, we saw lots of students* and *After the summer, both of us can study …* which just lift it above Band 3. The errors are generally non-impeding and little effort is required from the reader.

Band: 4

Part 1 – *Extra material*

1 B: 4 people on the beach; C: 2 people in the sea
2 9.15; 10.15; 10.30
3 sweater, cap, drink, notepad
4 picnic by castle, boat trip on river
5 6
6 skiing, walking, cycling
7 guitar, keyboard, singing

Part 1 – *Exam material*

1 A   2 B   3 C   4 B   5 A   6 A   7 C

Part 2 – *Extra material* (suggested answers)

2 football match
3 eating after football / beach party
4 travel arrangements / Sunday picnic
5 what to bring
6 what to do

Part 2 – *Exam material*

8 B   9 C   10 C   11 B   12 A   13 C

Part 3 – *Exam material*

14 (about) 7,500 (people) / (about) seven and a half thousand people / (about) 7.5 thousand
15 (small) H/hotel (business)   16 C/carrot(s)
17 B/boat(s)   18 G/garden   19 M/museum(s)

Part 4 – *Extra material*

1a   2a   3b   4b   5a   6b

Part 4 – *Exam material*

20 B   21 B   22 A   23 A   24 A   25 B

Transcript

This is the Cambridge Preliminary English Test, Test 1.

There are four parts to the test. You will hear each part twice. For each part of the test, there will be time for you to look through the questions and time for you to check your answers.

*Write your answers on the **question** paper. You will have six minutes at the end of the test to **copy your answers onto the answer sheet**.*

The recording will now be stopped.

Please ask any questions now, because you must not speak during the test.

PART 1

Now open your question paper and look at Part One.

There are seven questions in this part. For each question there are three pictures and a short recording. Choose the correct picture and put a tick in the box below it.

Before we start, here is an example.

Where did the man leave his camera?

Man: Oh no! I haven't got my camera!
Woman: But you used it just now to take a photograph of the fountain.
Man: Oh, I remember, I put it down on the steps while I put my coat on.
Woman: Well, let's drive back quickly – it might still be there.

The first picture is correct so there is a tick in box A.

Look at the three pictures for question 1 now.

Now we are ready to start. Listen carefully. You will hear each recording twice.

One.

What is the woman's first memory?

Woman: The first thing I remember is when I was about five my father took me to the seaside. My brother stayed at home with my mother because he was too young. We couldn't go in the sea because it was too rough, but we spent hours playing on the sand.

Now listen again.

Two.

Which train will the woman catch?

Woman: What time's the next train to Manchester please?
Man: You've just missed the 8.15. The next one's not until 10.15. There isn't one at 9.15.
Woman: But that's a two hour wait! and I'll be late for my appointment at 10.30. But I suppose I haven't any choice – I'll go for a coffee while I'm waiting.

Now listen again.

Three.

What should the students take with them tomorrow?

Teacher: Now, about the school picnic – it'll be hot so leave your sweaters behind but make sure you've got something to keep the sun off your head, and a drink in case you get thirsty … oh, and something to write on – that's for a game we're going to play. And don't be late!

Now listen again.

Four.

What will they do at the weekend?

Woman: What shall we do at the weekend, Tony? The Browns are coming up with their children. I was wondering about a visit to the zoo, or a river trip … or just going down to the sea again …

Man: Let's do something different. The weather should be good, so we could take a picnic to the castle instead. The children will enjoy it and it'll be a nice change from the beach.

Woman: Right then, we'll do that.

Now listen again.

Five.

What does the woman need to buy?

Woman: Let me see, eggs – I've got lots of those; butter – I don't need that. I'll get some milk, bread, and I've nearly finished the toothpaste … oh, there's a new one in the cupboard. But I do need some apples. Now, where's my purse?

Now listen again.

Six.

How will the boy get to school?

Woman: Get up, Martin. It's snowed during the night. The school bus won't be able to go, so you'll have to walk.

Boy: Oh, I'll go by bike.

Woman: Don't be silly. The snow's far too deep for that.

Boy: Then I'll ski. That'll be quicker than walking and I can save the bus fare! But I'll have some breakfast first.

Now listen again.

Seven.

Which is Tanya's boyfriend?

Woman 1: Look – this is the band on the television now, Tanya's boyfriend is the singer.

Woman 2: She told me he played the guitar.

Woman 1: He does sometimes, but not tonight, and you know he used to be the keyboard player in that other band. He's so brilliant. Don't you think she's lucky?

Woman 2: Oh, I don't know. I think I prefer the drummer myself, actually.

Now listen again.

That is the end of Part One.

Now turn to Part Two, questions 8 to 13.

PART 2

You will hear a teacher talking to a group of students.

For each question, put a tick in the correct box.

You now have 45 seconds to look at the questions for Part Two.

Now we are ready to start. Listen carefully. You will hear the recording twice.

Teacher: And now I'd like to tell you about some of the activities that we've arranged for your last weekend. Now that the course is finished, you can relax and I think you'll be very interested in what we've got planned.

As usual, tonight is Friday night down at Sam's Disco. Tonight's going to be a bit special, not because it's your last weekend, but because Sam is 30 today, and he'll be having a big party down there. So – from eight thirty this evening, Sam's Disco will be the place to be and it's half-price before ten thirty.

Now, for those of you who are interested in football, we've arranged a football match against the students of Henry's College. We usually hold the match on the beach but this time it'll be in South Park. If you're a footballer, go there at two o'clock tomorrow. It's opposite the new Sports Centre and it isn't difficult to find. Afterwards, we thought we'd all get together – both colleges. We tried to book the local pizza restaurant but unfortunately they couldn't take more than about twelve people. Instead we've decided to have a beach party. We'll meet back at the college and set off together at about five o'clock. We've managed to persuade a couple of guitarists from the local pub to come and entertain us.

Sunday will be the last social event and we're having a picnic in Thornton Forest. Everybody should meet at the college at twelve fifteen. We'll walk to the station and take the quarter to one train to Thornton. It's about a twenty-minute train ride and then a short walk to the forest. And it looks like we're going to be lucky with the weather. The teachers will bring all the food – chicken, salad, bread rolls and plates and things like that. Everybody seems to have their favourite drink these days so we'd like you to provide that. Don't worry about the glasses though – we'll bring along some plastic cups.

There's a small lake in the middle of the forest which we always visit. It's not deep enough to swim in, nor are there any fish there. But it is very beautiful so do bring your cameras. It's lovely just to sit and relax by the water after walking there.

We'll return home before it gets dark so we should get back at about six thirty. Now, are there any questions …

Now listen again.

That is the end of Part Two.

Now turn to Part Three, questions 14 to 19.

PART 3

You will hear someone who lives in Lidsey talking on the radio.

For each question, fill in the missing information in the numbered space.

You now have 20 seconds to look at Part Three.

Now we are ready to start. Listen carefully. You will hear the recording twice.

Interviewer: For those who don't know the area, tell us something about Lidsey.

Woman: Well, I've lived there for 10 years. It's a small town with a population of about seven and a half thousand. We decided to move from London and were looking for a small business to buy. We thought that Lidsey looked like a nice town to live in. The streets are full of small, friendly shops – food shops, antique shops and the usual banks and offices. In the end we bought a small hotel in the centre which was built in 1368, so it's got quite a history. It needed a lot of work but it's now a very successful business.

The special thing about Lidsey is the wide main street that used to have an open waterway in it. Boats used to come right into the town centre to transport food grown in the area, mainly potatoes and carrots, from Lidsey down to London by boat. The

waterway was filled in years ago and now it's a wide street, as I say. There isn't much industry in the area now, but there is a small company down by the river which builds boats.

In the old days, the family who owned most of the town lived in a large house near the centre. Unfortunately the house was pulled down about ten years ago. But part of the garden is now open to the public, and people come from miles around to visit it.

We've also got one of the best museums in the area which is in the old Town Hall. There are a lot of different rooms furnished as they used to be in the old days, and it's open from April to September on Thursday and Sunday afternoons.

Interviewer: Well, thank you, it sounds an interesting place.

Now listen again.

That is the end of Part Three.

Now turn to Part Four, questions 20 to 25.

PART 4

Look at the six sentences for this part. You will hear a conversation between a girl, Mary, and her father, about computers.

Decide if each sentence is correct or incorrect. If it is correct, put a tick in the box under A for YES. If it is not correct, put a tick in the box under B for NO.

You now have 20 seconds to look at the questions for Part 4.

Now we are ready to start. Listen carefully. You will hear the recording twice.

Father: Mary, could you come and help me for a moment please?

Mary: Okay, Dad. Just coming … What's the matter?

Father: It's the computer, Mary. Every time I turn it on there seems to be another problem.

Mary: Let's see … looks okay to me Dad … I'll just start the program … yes, there you are. Nothing wrong.

Father: Thanks Mary. I really don't know how I'd use this machine at all without your help. You're so quick at everything …

Mary: Well Dad, I've been able to use a computer since I was four, so of course it's not difficult. It's easy to learn things when you're a child. It's like learning to ride a bike, once you can do it you never forget.

Father: True. I've tried reading the instructions for the computer – they seem very confusing – *you* can probably understand them but *I* certainly can't.

Mary: I don't find them easy to follow either – what they say is really unclear. The best way is to just sit down and use it.

Father: That's my difficulty, I think – there just weren't any computers when I was young, so I haven't learnt to use one properly. It's too late to learn now.

Mary: Don't be silly, Dad. There are lots of people of your age in computer classes.

Father: Do you really think so?

Mary: Yes, really.

Father: Right, I'll try and find a class in the evenings, or perhaps a weekend course. Could you help me finish *this* piece of work, though?

Mary: Of course … you know, talking about this has given me an idea for a special report I've got to do as part of my social studies class. I could find out when they started teaching computer skills in schools. I could start with England, and then compare what happened here with what happened in other countries. What do you think?

Father: Sounds interesting.

Now listen again.

That is the end of Part Four.

You now have six minutes to check and copy your answers onto the answer sheet.

You have one more minute.

That is the end of the test.

PAPER 3 ● Speaking

Part 2 – Extra material (sample answer)

Cameras and diary are good because he can record his experiences.

He'll definitely need clothes – and different ones for different weather.

I don't think a car or bike is important because he can rent one.

The toothpaste is good because he doesn't want to spend money on that – it's better to bring it with him.

He'll probably need some sports equipment like his tennis racket because he likes playing tennis.

For me, the most important thing is the money – he can't do anything without that.

Parts 3 and 4 – Extra material

Part 3: they are; having / eating; There; is pouring; is putting / spreading; is having / has got; is / looks; can see; behind

Part 4: Students' own answers.

TEST 2

PAPER 1 ● Reading and Writing

Reading

Part 1 – Extra material

Question 1: 1 B 2 tell
Question 2: 1 B
Question 3: 1 B 2 is busy / crowded 3 must
Question 4: 1 Greg ✔ 2 Dave ✔ 3 Kim ✘
   4 Ben ✘

Question 5: 1 B 2 The shop wants / asks customers to show a copy of the repair form at the time they collect their computer.

Part 1 – Exam material

1 B 2 A 3 B 4 C 5 A

Part 2 – Extra material

Henry: management studies; modern; city centre; —; college for 1st year

Anna: physics; sports facilities; city centre; —; —

Philip: education; modern sports facilities; countryside; —; —

Monica: German; sports facilities; —; part-time; no

Part 2 – Exam material

6 D   7 C   8 F   9 H   10 A

Part 3 – Extra material

Question 13: at sunset – text says in the early morning

Question 14: when people speak too loudly

Question 15: there is always the possibility that you may be very unlucky and not see certain animals.

Question 17: you have to pay a small booking fee

Question 18: no, the text says that no special skills are needed

Question 20: 12

Part 3 – Exam material

11 A   12 A   13 B   14 B   15 B   16 A   17 B
18 B   19 A   20 B

Part 4 – Extra material

1   Ruth Black's

2   it's no longer traditional to sing together

3   we think we can't; we've forgotten what we learned as children

4   a) It brings people together; b) encourages good breathing; people become more confident and learn to control stress

5   a friend told her about it

6   because she enjoyed singing so much

7   no; all singers can go

Question 21: the writer describes

Question 22: Everyone is able to sing

Question 23: But more than anything

Question 24: … an excellent singing class and became so keen that she started …

Question 25: A No   B No   C Yes   D No

Part 4 – Exam material

21 B   22 A   23 C   24 D   25 C

Part 5 – Exam material

26 C   27 B   28 D   29 D   30 A   31 B   32 A
33 B   34 B   35 C

Part 1 – Extra material

it's not necessary – you don't need to

suggested – why not

I was given – he gave me

not far – quite near

is very popular – everyone likes

how much – the cost

it'd be good if – I really ought to

since last year – a year ago

not many – a few

Part 1 – Exam material

1   few / couple of / small number of

2   you show me

3   don't you / we // not

4   to go

5   price of / cost of // fee for

Part 2 – Sample answers

Task-specific Mark Scheme

* send your **congratulations**
* question(s) about **the baby**
* information about **present candidate is sending**

Question 6: email to couple
Sample Answer A

Hi Just mam and dad!!!
CONGRATULATIONS!!! It's fantastic … you have a son!
How is David? Is he like his mam or like his dad? Of course, he is very nice! What do you think if I send him a photographic album! It's an original present!
    Love,
        Mathilde

Examiner's comments

Although this script is not perfect, all three content elements are covered and the message is clearly communicated.

Band: 5

Sample Answer B

> *Hello, I decide to write you this email, because I've known that your baby was born. I am very happy for you. It must be fantastick to have a baby. How is he like? Has he red hair like you, Rob? Is he irritable like Clara? I'm funny. However, Congratulations!*
>
> *From Gloria with love*

Examiner's comments

Two content elements are covered satisfactorily, but the third, the present for the baby, is omitted.

Band: 3

Part 3 – Sample answers

Question 7: letter to a friend
Sample Answer A

> *Dear Bob,*
> *My favorite sport has always been swimming. I love it!*
> *I started swimming when I was 10, and never stopped till last year when I started university. I believe it is the m ost complete sport for training the body and that it is one of the few sports where you can't win if you don't pratice a lot.*
> *Unfortunatly I had to stop swimming because I didn't have time to practice 2 hours every day. I also love competitions: it is great when you have to race with someone else, and it is even better when you finish your race and find out you have improved your best time.*
> *Yours*
> *Andrea*

Examiner's comments

This is a very good attempt, showing confident and ambitious language, for example *My favorite sport has always been swimming*. It is very well organised, with a wide range of structures and vocabulary, for example *it is one of the few sports where you can't win if you don't pratice a lot*. The few minor errors in spelling do not detract from the high degree of accuracy.

Band: 5

Sample Answer B

> *Hi; my friend*
> *I want to answer at yours asking; my favourite sportt is football, it's a great team sport; in this sport there are abilities; strong; team play; and like all things in life there is a fortune in certain case. Football is much playing in my country; here in Italy football is really a great part of all us; I love it really, but, my football team unluckly don't go well in this season. But I hope that it's return a great team someday. Hello for now; we can playing football together someday you know?*

Examiner's comments

This is an inadequate attempt, with limited language and inadequate range. The erratic punctuation adds to the incoherence, for example *in this sport there are abilities; strong; team play; …* The numerous errors sometimes impede, for example *I want to answer at yours asking* and considerable effort is required from the reader.

Band: 2

Question 8: The bus was late so I decided to walk
Sample Answer C

> *The bus was late so I decided to walk. That day I had a lesson. During my walk I met my friend Claudia. We didn't meet each other for long time so I decided to go with her in a bar. She was very down because her boyfriend was away for a work. I wanted to help her and so I suggested to go to disco that evening. So we went to Jubilee and she enjoied herself too much. So I was very happy and she too because that evening she met a lot of her old friend and so for few hour didn't remind her boyfriend.*

Examiner's comments

This adequate attempt shows some ambition but it is flawed, for example *I suggested to go to disco*. There is an adequate range of structures and some simple linking, for example *During my walk I met my friend.* A number of errors, for example *so for few hour didn't remind her boyfriend* require some effort from the reader.

Band: 3

Sample Answer D

> The bus was late so I decided to walk, there was noone in the streets and the wind was freezing my hands, when the tower of the church began to bang I started running. Although the fast movements the cold sensation seemed to be stronger. Little by little I began hearing noises from every corner of the road without seeing anything. Those well-known streets began to seem so unknown and frightening. After a few minutes I realized I got lost a I desidered I've never left the bus-stop but suddenly I saw in the darkness a black shadow standing in front of me at the end of the road. I immediately stopped but the shadow started running towards me, I was paralized by the cold and the fear, I hit something with my left leg and I fell off over a sack of rubbish, I had never felt the death so close ...

Examiner's comments

This is a good attempt with a wide range and ambitious use of language, for example *Little by little, without seeing anything* and *the wind was freezing my hands.* There is evidence of organisation and quite good linking. However the accuracy is not sufficient for a Band 5, for example *I desidered I've never left the bus-stop.*

Band: 4

PAPER 2 ● Listening

Part 1 – Extra material

Question 1: tomorrow

Question 2: first

Question 3: with the bread in the bag; with the fruit; in the pie

Question 4: in B he's giving her the books and the bike is on the floor; in C he's holding the bike and she's picking up the books

Question 5: hair, clothes, glasses and age

Question 6: twenty to eleven; ten to eleven; ten past eleven

Question 7: old city / buildings; church in countryside with mountains; people on beach

Part 1 – Exam material

1 A   2 C   3 B   4 B   5 C   6 B   7 A

Part 2 – Exam material

8 A   9 B   10 B   11 C   12 C   13 B

Part 3 – Extra material

students' own answers

Part 3 – Exam material

14    $9\frac{1}{2}$ / 9.5 / 9/nine and (a) half (hours) / nine hours thirty minutes

15   rain

16   D/deck 6 / six

17   S/snack(s)

18   M/magic

19   B/bookshop

Part 4 – Extra material

1 her father's colleague
2 She'd like to work in South America one day.
3 St Petersburg
4 England
5 He didn't have time.
6 He's sorry. It would be good for his business.
7 It's a long way from home.
8 about 20
9 yes (Her Mum always wanted to see the Great Wall of China.)
10 yes

Part 4 – Exam material

20 B   21 A   22 A   23 B   24 B   25 A

Transcript

This is the Cambridge Preliminary English Test, Test 2.

There are four parts to the test. You will hear each part twice. For each part of the test there will be time for you to look through the questions and time for you to check your answers.

Write your answers on the **question** paper. You will have six minutes at the end of the test to **copy your answers onto the answer sheet**.

The recording will now be stopped.

Please ask any questions now, because you must not speak during the test.

PART 1

Now open your question paper and look at Part One.

There are seven questions in this part. For each question there are three pictures and a short recording. Choose the correct picture and put a tick in the box below it.

Before we start, here is an example.

Where did the man leave his camera?

Man: Oh no! I haven't got my camera!
Woman: But you used it just now to take a photograph of the fountain.
Man: Oh I remember, I put it down on the steps while I put my coat on.
Woman: Well, let's drive back quickly – it might still be there.

The first picture is correct so there is a tick in box A.

Look at the three pictures for question 1 now.

Now we are ready to start. Listen carefully. You will hear each recording twice.

One.

What will the weather be like tomorrow?

Announcer: Here is the weather forecast. Today will be very cloudy, although it won't rain until the evening. The weather tomorrow will be the same as yesterday – sunshine and showers. But the weekend looks good – plenty of sunshine and very little rain.

Now listen again.

Two.

What will the man do first?

Woman: Steve, what are you going to do today?
Man: Mmm ... well, I've got to have my hair cut, but before I do anything I need to ring Peter and see if he wants to play golf.
Woman: That's a good idea, you haven't played for a while, have you?

Now listen again.

Three.

Where's the knife?

Woman: I'm glad we decided to stop here for our picnic. Can you find the knife for me, and I'll cut up the cucumber? I packed it in the bag with the bread ... oh, but I used it to peel some oranges when we stopped in the petrol station so it'll be with them. I hope it's big enough to cut up this pie.

Now listen again.

Four.

What happened to the girl this afternoon?

Girl: You'll never guess what happened to me this afternoon! I was cycling over the bridge in town, when there was this really strong wind, and I fell off my bike. I didn't hurt myself, but my books were thrown onto the pavement and went everywhere. This really nice boy picked them up for me! It's lucky there were no cars around to drive over my bike, which was still in the road. I thanked the boy, then I picked up my bike and cycled away. I was ...

Now listen again.

Five.

Which man is waiting at the bus stop?

Boy: Oh look, that's my new English teacher over there, see – he's waiting at the bus stop.

Girl: The young one with sunglasses and blond hair? You always told me your teacher was bald and really old and got angry because he kept losing his glasses.

Boy: That was the teacher I had before. This one is really nice.

Now listen again.

Six.

What time does the television programme end?

Mum: Go to bed, Luke. It's already twenty to eleven and you've got to be up early in the morning.

Boy: Aw, mum, just another few minutes. I'm watching this brilliant TV programme about American football. It'll be over at 10 to and I can be in bed by 10 past. Nobody in my class has to go to bed before 11 o'clock. It's not fair.

Now listen again.

Seven.

Which postcard will they send to Mark?

Man: I'm getting this postcard of that bridge in the old city for my parents. And this church looks nice – shall we send it to Mark? He likes old buildings.

Woman: But we haven't actually been there – we should send him a card of something we've actually seen. Here's the beach we went to yesterday.

Man: But it looks horrible and crowded in that picture.

Woman: Oh, just get him the same one as you're sending to your parents.

Now listen again.

That is the end of Part One.

Now turn to Part Two, questions 8 to 13.

PART 2

You will hear a young man called Toby Wood talking on the radio about what it's like to work in the kitchen of a famous chef.

For each question, put a tick in the correct box.

You now have 45 seconds to look at the questions for Part Two.

Now we are ready to start. Listen carefully. You will hear the recording twice.

Int: The young chef Toby Wood recently worked for three days in the kitchen of the well-known chef, Oliver Rix. Toby, what was it like?

Toby: It was a strange experience for me because when I finished college six years ago, I promised myself that one day I'd work with Oliver because I think he's an excellent chef. I was quite nervous about going to work in his restaurant kitchen. But I loved it when I got there, although his team of young cooks are very busy and there isn't time to sit around and chat.

At 7 a.m. when I started in the kitchen, I couldn't believe how quiet it was. The food preparation is very important, and on my first morning I cut vegetables. I had two problems. Cooking in professional kitchens is lovely when you know where things are. But I had to be told where everything was. Also, I didn't cut the vegetables as Oliver wanted. In Oliver's kitchen, you do things his way.

Oliver has little tests for new chefs. One is the way you prepare the biscuits. There are seven different kinds and two of each kind are served with coffee. Oliver believes that an intelligent chef will decorate them beautifully and then put them in pairs on the plate. I'm glad to say I passed that test!

Oliver is very calm in the kitchen, and doesn't get angry very often. However, when it comes to putting food on the customers' plates, every second counts. The only time Oliver shouts is when that goes wrong. Each table's plates have to go out together, and if everything isn't ready, he'll just throw the whole lot away!

Oliver's family have put cash into the business, so it's important that it's successful. I spoke to the kitchen staff to find out what they think about Oliver. They all say he's an excellent boss. When he shouts at them, they say it's for a good reason. In return for their hard work, they are well paid, and they learn a lot from him.

When Oliver's young cooks have been with him for a few years, he likes to send them to the best restaurants in France to get more experience. Most realise it's a good idea, and will do that for a few months. They also know that when they've finished training, he'll help them start their own restaurants. Even after they leave his restaurant, he continues to give advice.

Now listen again.

That is the end of Part Two.

Now turn to Part Three, questions 14 to 19.

PART 3

You will hear someone talking to passengers on a boat from England to France.

For each question, fill in the missing information in the numbered space.

You now have 20 seconds to look at Part Three.

Now we are ready to start. Listen carefully. You will hear the recording twice.

Woman: Good morning everyone and welcome on board our ferry, the Queen Isabel, which is taking you from Portsmouth to St Malo in France.

Today our trip will last nine and a half hours and we should arrive in St Malo at 10 past 6 this evening, local time.

Now, for the weather forecast. Unfortunately the rain is unlikely to stop. So only the bravest of you will feel like going onto our outside decks.

I must now ask you to listen carefully to these instructions, which you should follow in an emergency. If you hear the ship's alarm signal, which is a number of short whistles, go to the lounge on Deck 6. There, a member of staff will tell you what to do.

We have several restaurants on board serving a variety of meals and snacks. Lunch and dinner with waiter service are served in the Ocean Grill on Deck 3. This opens at 11.30. You can get snacks and drinks in the Captain's Café, also on Deck 3, from 10.30.

For your entertainment on board today the ship's cinema is showing a children's film at 11 o'clock. And at 12.30 adults can see the adventure film *Dangerous Dream*. At 3.30, also for children, we have a magic show in the Children's Play Centre.

During the voyage, don't forget to visit the shops on Deck 3. There is a duty-free shop, a clothes boutique and a bookshop which sells postcards and stamps as well as books and newspapers.

Our staff are ready to help you at all times. Please ask if you need anything. We hope you enjoy the voyage.

Now listen again.

That is the end of Part Three.

Now turn to Part Four, questions 20 to 25.

PART 4

Look at the six sentences for this part. You will hear a conversation between a girl, Charlotte, and her father about what she's going to study next year.

Decide if each sentence is correct or incorrect. If it is correct, put a tick in the box under A for YES. If it is not correct, put a tick in the box under B for NO.

You now have 20 seconds to look at the questions for Part Four.

Now we are ready to start. Listen carefully. You will hear the recording twice.

Father: Have you decided which languages you're going to do at college next year Charlotte?

Charlotte: Well, as you know, I really want to study Spanish ...

Father: Mmm ... a colleague of mine is studying Spanish. He speaks French and German too, and he says he's found Spanish grammar the easiest to learn.

Charlotte: Well ... that's not the reason I want to study it. Spanish is an important world language you know, and I'd like to work in South America one day.

Father: I see. And what about the other language? You're going to do two, aren't you? Have you thought about Russian? Your grandmother would be delighted ...

Charlotte: I know she would. Her parents were born in St Petersburg, weren't they?

Father: Yes, but they came to England just before your grandmother was born ...

Charlotte: Well, anyway, I don't think I'm going to do Russian. I think I'd like to do Chinese.

Father: Really? I wanted to learn Chinese when I was younger, but sadly I didn't have time. It would be really useful now for my business to be able to speak it.

Charlotte: Oh, it's a fantastic language isn't it? And the course sounds really good. I'll have the chance to spend six months actually studying the language in China.

Father: It seems a very long way away ... I'll worry about you being thousands of kilometres from home ...

Charlotte: Come on, Dad. I really like the idea. There'll be so much to see and do, and I wouldn't be on my own. There'd be a whole group of students going out together – about 20 each year.

Father:	Oh, I see ... but all the same ... it's a long way.
Charlotte:	And perhaps you and Mum could come out for a holiday while I was there ... Mum's always wanted to see the 'Great Wall of China'.
Father:	Yes, she has ... we'll have to talk about it when she gets in, won't we?
Charlotte:	Great idea, Dad.

Now listen again.

That is the end of Part Four.

You now have six minutes to check and copy your answers on to the answer sheet.

You have one more minute.

That is the end of the test.

TEST 3

PAPER 1 ● Reading and Writing

Reading

Part 1 – Extra material

1 B, C
2 yes
3 a) Mum   b) in the fridge   c) flour
4 because staff are ill
5 through the letterbox
6 no
7 getting your train ready
8 queue
9 passengers who have got tickets

Part 1 – Exam material

1 C   2 A   3 B   4 C   5 C

Part 2 – Extra material

2 D is not suitable because there's no information about public transport.
3 D isn't suitable because there's no information about hotels.
4 B isn't suitable because Paolo doesn't have a car and there's no information about accommodation. E isn't suitable because there's not much practical information for the traveller.
5 B isn't suitable because we don't know if the places are tourist centres or less popular towns.

Part 2 – Exam material

6 F   7 H   8 A   9 G   10 C

Part 3 – Extra material

Question 11: yes, 'fastest growing'
Question 12: no, it says 'up to'
Question 13: 'the top service provider in the country'
Question 14: yes, 'please let us know which card you'll be using.'
Question 15: no, receiving a text message is free.
Question 16: 20p per minute; yes, 'calls ... are charged by the second.'
Question 17: yes, 'to remind you of important dates'
Question 18: 'change your message' and 'whenever you like'
Question 19: to record a message; you are given instructions to follow
Question 20: more than one time period; you choose

Part 3 – Exam material

11 A   12 B   13 A   14 A   15 B   16 B   17 A
18 A   19 A   20 B

Part 4 – Extra material

1 He bought a house and made his own CD recording.
2 He planned to save the money and retire.
3 No, he didn't.
4 He fell in love with the beautiful sound it made.
5 No, she says she's pleased for him.
6 Because he wouldn't be happy retiring. He loves music too much.
7 He's still playing.

Question 21: A he tells us   B yes   C he tells us   D nowhere

Question 22: no

Question 23: No, she does talk about him and money generally but not about what he did with this money.

Question 24: no

Question 25: A no   B no   C no

Part 4 – Exam material

21 B   22 C   23 D   24 A   25 D

Part 5 – Exam material

26 B   27 D   28 D   29 A   30 B   31 B   32 D
33 C   34 A   35 C

Writing

Part 1 – Extra material

1 younger
2 Because
3 'become'
4 past simple
5 'a'
6 a singer
7 more famous

Part 1 – Exam material

1 younger   2 because / as / since   3 became
4 singer   5 (much) more famous / well-known

Part 2 – Extra material

Pierre didn't include why he chose the postcard for Chris and he didn't ask about the weather in Australia. His answer is not very good.

Part 2 – Exam material

Question 6: postcard to Chris

See sample answer from Pierre on page 69.

Examiner's comments

Only one content element ('say something about the gallery') is included; the candidate did not include the other two. Therefore the message is only partly communicated.

Band: 2

Task-specific Mark Scheme

- information about **the gallery**
- explanation about **choice of postcard**
- question about **the weather in Australia**

Sample Answer A

> Hello Chris
> Today I visited art-gallery. I was fantastic, I like it. The exhabition was about modern art, so I thought you like it and I choosen for you a post card This is art of young man; he is from Australia. So Chris how was the weather in Australia?

Examiner's comments

In this script, all three content elements are adequately dealt with and the message is communicated successfully, on the whole, although the language errors require some effort by the reader.

Band: 4

Part 3 – Extra material

Question 7: 1 It's OK.   2 Yes, it does.
   3 Yes. There are quite a few mistakes which make it difficult to understand.

Part 3 – Exam material

Question 7: letter to a friend

See sample answer from Abdul on page 70.

Examiner's comments

This is an adequate attempt, showing some ambitious language but with flaws, for example *I don't know if he like music or not, but will be surprise if you buy any CD*. There is adequate range and organisation but a number of mostly non-impeding errors, especially in the second paragraph, for example *If your brother like futbooll you can buy for him a booll so he can enjoy playen ...* Some effort by the reader is required here.

Band: 3

Sample Answer A

> Hello Stefanie,
> I cam help you. I think for your brother's
> his like the playgames exempel because my
> brother's like this and the short car the
> collection. In my country don't have the
> special things but I think for your choice
> depend the him like. Your know his now
> your have my idea and the other is bought
> ticket for see him the favorite star, he like
> the singing or the star? but we've going to
> the shopping toghether one day for exempel
> on twenty-height march I think is better
> because we' have the lot of time for cherche
> one present for your brother's. I'm happy
> your write my about this,
> And see you soon.
> Love Anne

Examiner's comments

This script displays a severely restricted command of language, in which any evidence of range of structure or vocabulary is obscured by very poor control, for example ... *his like the playgames exempel because* ... and *your choice depend the him like.* It is difficult to understand and requires excessive effort by the reader.

Band: 1

Part 3 – Extra material

Question 8: As, Suddenly, When, Then, and, By the time, and, and, At first, but then

Question 8: A very unusual evening

See sample answer page 70.

Examiner's comments

This is a very good attempt, showing confident and ambitious use of language, for example *As I had plenty of time I was walking slowly.* There is a wide range of structures and vocabulary, for example *Without a second thought I sprung into the river.* Good use of linking devices makes it well organised and coherent. Although there are a few minor non-impeding errors, for example *One of them pushed the other down the bridge,* no effort is required by the reader.

Band: 5

Sample Answer B

> A very unusual evening
> It was happened when I lived in my
> country. One day told me friend of mine
> that he has a friend who is a forester. He
> invited him to your hunting evening and
> he asked me if I want to join him. I decided
> say yes becose I have never seen it before. We
> went to forest by car. Then we went by walk
> some milers.
> Suddenly we stoped and

Examiner's comments

This inadequate and limited attempt lacks cohesion, due to the numerous language errors which impede communication, for example *One day told me friend of mine* ... Considerable effort is required from the reader, not least to sort out the personal pronouns. This script appears unfinished and there are only 70 words here, which means it is limited to a maximum Band 4. However, since the language does not achieve this anyway, there is no further penalty.

Band: 2

Part 1 – Extra material

Question 1: scarf, perfume, chocolates

Question 2: His sister probably and in picture C, his mother probably.

Question 3: 'next'

Question 4: 'now'

Question 5: quarter past three (3.15); five o'clock (5.00); twenty past five (5.20); 'ready'

Question 6: music, tennis, wildlife / animals

Question 7: plane, train, car

Part 1 – Exam material

1 A   2 C   3 C   4 B   5 C   6 B   7 A

Part 2 – Extra material

Question 8: 1 secretary   2 bank clerk
3 travel agent   4 sportswear designer

Question 9: design & make clothes Year 2; history of fashion Year 1; work in a big store Year 3

Question 10: her Mum and Dad

Question 11: No; because the clothes feel soft when you've got them on

Question 12: a few; most of them

Question 13: No

Part 2 – Exam material

8 C   9 B   10 A   11 C   12 C   13 A

Part 3 – Extra material

14 a day

15 a number

16 maps / information / brochures etc.

17 gate / entrance

18 walking / swimming etc.

19 snack / talk etc.

Part 3 – Exam material

14 (is open) T/Tuesday (to S/Sunday)

15 109/one hundred and nine

16 M/map(s)

17 (park) E/entrance (to the park)

18 F/fishing (on the lake)

19 T/talk

Part 4 – Exam material

20 A   21 B   22 A   23 B   24 A   25 A

Transcript

This is the Cambridge Preliminary English Test, Test 3.

There are four parts to the test. You will hear each part twice. For each part of the test there will be time for you to look through the questions and time for you to check your answers.

*Write your answers on the **question paper**. You will have six minutes at the end of the test to **copy your answers onto the answer sheet**.*

The recording will now be stopped.

Please ask any questions now, because you must not speak during the test.

PART 1

Now open your question paper and look at Part One.

There are seven questions in this part. For each question there are three pictures and a short recording. Choose the correct picture and put a tick in the box below it.

Before we start, here is an example.

Where did the man leave his camera?

Man: Oh no! I haven't got my camera!

Woman: But you used it just now to take a photograph of the fountain.

Man: Oh I remember, I put it down on the steps while I put my coat on.

Woman: Well, let's drive back quickly – it might still be there.

The first picture is correct so there is a tick in box A.

Look at the three pictures for question 1 now.

Now we are ready to start. Listen carefully. You will hear each recording twice.

One.

Which present will the girl take?

Girl: I really don't know what to give Mrs Allemano when I go and stay with her in New York. Do you think she'd like some perfume?

Man: Well, you don't know her very well, do you, so I'd choose something like a scarf, or just a box of chocolates.

Girl: Umm ... I like your first idea best – it'll be much easier to carry.

Now listen again.

Two.

Who lives in Joe's house now?

Woman: Does your house seem empty now your sister's left home, Joe?

Man: Not really. My grandmother's moved into her room, and she doesn't go out much. It's really nice having her there because my father never comes home until late, and if my mother's out for the evening, grandma cooks supper for me.

Now listen again.

Three.

Who will be on the stage next?

Man: And that was *Fever*, with Adam on piano and Gus on guitar. Lots of music to come, including the *3 Shore Sisters* with songs from their new CD. But first, here are *The Cotton Seeds* – you all know the drummer and guitarist, but singing here with them for the first time is Jenny Lo, the drummer's sister – please give her a big welcome.

Now listen again.

Four.

Where is the woman's notebook now?

Woman: Excuse me, waiter. I think I left my notebook on this table – have you seen it? It's red.

Waiter: Oh yes. I took it inside with the empty glasses when I cleared the table. I gave it to the manager, who put it with the other lost property. He keeps it all in the drawer of his desk.

Woman: I see. Where is he now?

Waiter: He's on the phone inside the café. Why don't you go inside – he'll be finished in a minute.

Now listen again.

Five.

What time will the cake be ready?

Girl: What time is it, Mum?

Mother: 4.35.

Girl: And the cake went into the oven at quarter past three?

Mother: That's right. You could check it at five, but don't take it out until twenty past. That's 45 minutes to go!

Now listen again.

Six.

Which TV programme will they watch together?

Woman: Hasn't that tennis match finished yet? You know I want to watch the wild life programme at 9 o'clock.

Man: It's cancelled, and everything's running late because the pop concert finished later than expected. Sit down and watch this match with me. It's really exciting, and more interesting than looking at animals.

Woman: Oh, OK then.

Now listen again.

Seven.

How will the family get to Glasgow?

Woman: Hello Mum ... we'll be with you on Tuesday ... No, the train's almost as expensive as flying and takes much longer. We're doing as I said we would ... We land in Glasgow at 4 o'clock ... and then we'll hire a car to drive to your house ...

Now listen again.

That is the end of Part One.

Now turn to Part Two, questions 8 to 13.

PART 2

You will hear Louise Bright telling some students about her work as a clothes designer.

For each question, put a tick in the correct box.

You now have 45 seconds to look at the questions for Part Two.

Now we are ready to start. Listen carefully. You will hear the recording twice.

Louise: Good evening everyone, my name's Louise Bright. I've worked as a sportswear designer for a big store for four years now, but I haven't always worked in fashion. When I left school I worked as a secretary for a couple of years, and then became a bank clerk before getting a job in a travel agency. But I always dreamt about working in fashion, and I used to spend a lot of time staring out of the window and drawing clothes!

So, when I was 25, I went to college – the London School of Fashion, and did a four-year course there. You don't learn how to actually design and make clothes until the second year – the first year is spent looking back at the fashions of the past. In the third year you work in a big store, looking at clothes made by all the famous fashion names.

I enjoyed the last year of the course most, because each student designs seven sets of clothes for the final fashion show. All the students at the school come to the final show, and you can invite other friends as well. But for me, the best thing was that my Mum and Dad could come and see what I'd done. Of course, people who are really well-known in the fashion trade often come too.

I loved the final show. The things I designed were all sports clothes. The shape of these clothes is really quite simple, so it's sometimes hard to make them look new and interesting. But I particularly like the materials you use because they feel soft when you've got them on.

I was very lucky to get work as a fashion designer as soon as I'd finished college. A few students from my course were offered work by really famous fashion designers, but I was offered permanent work by the store I'd worked for as a student, and I'm now designing a special range of clothes for the store. In fact, most of the other students on my course aren't designing at all – they're working in advertising for the fashion industry.

I really love my work, but I intend to have my own business in the end – I'd like to design children's sports clothes, and sell them on the internet. I don't expect to be fantastically successful, but if I could earn enough to live on, that would be great.

Now listen again.

That is the end of Part Two.

Now turn to Part Three, questions 14 to 19.

PART 3

You will hear a recorded message about Finchbrooke Country Park.

For each question, fill in the missing information in the numbered space.

You now have 20 seconds to look at Part Three.

Now we are ready to start. Listen carefully. You will hear the recording twice.

Man: Finchbrooke Country Park is open seven days a week, from 8 a.m. to 7 p.m. The Visitors' Centre is open Tuesday to Sunday, between 9 a.m. and 5.30 p.m. The café, which is next to the Visitors'

Centre, is open from 10 a.m. to 5 p.m., Wednesday to Sunday.

The park is 10 miles north of Hampton, and there's a regular bus service to the park from the centre of the town, number 109, leaving every 15 minutes. For visitors coming by car, parking at Finchbrooke is free. There's a 20 miles per hour speed limit inside the park and all drivers are asked to keep to this.

At the Visitors' Centre, there's a wide selection of books and videos for sale and for no charge, maps are available. These show all the marked paths inside the park. There are many hard-surfaced paths which are suitable for pushchairs, wheelchairs and for walking in all weather.

There's a public telephone in the Visitors' Centre. In the event of an accident or emergency outside Visitor Centre opening hours, there is another phone at the park entrance.

There's a bike hire service at the park and it is also possible to go fishing on the lake and to camp in the forest. Further information about these activities is available from staff at the Visitors' Centre. Visitors are reminded that swimming and skating are not allowed on the lake.

Events can be arranged for groups and schools and bookings should be made with Visitors' Centre staff. The educational staff at the park are experienced with all ages. The group will hear a talk and then they will be taken on a guided tour.

Thank you for calling Finchbrooke Country Park.

Now listen again.

That is the end of Part Three.

Now turn to Part Four, questions 20 to 25.

PART 4

Look at the six sentences for this part. You will hear a conversation between a boy called Tony and a girl called Rachel, about watching television.

Decide if each sentence is correct or incorrect. If it is correct, put a tick in the box under A for YES. If it is not correct, put a tick in the box under B for NO.

You now have 20 seconds to look at the questions for Part Four.

Now we are ready to start. Listen carefully. You will hear the recording twice.

Tony: Hi Rachel, how are you?

Rachel: OK. Actually not really. Tell me, do you have a TV in your bedroom?

Tony: Yeah. I got one for my birthday last month; it's great.

Rachel: Oh you're lucky. My Mum won't let me have one.

Tony: Why not? It's much better because you avoid all those boring arguments about what to watch.

Rachel: Right. My sister always wants to watch lots of cartoons and I'm really not keen on them.

Tony: Exactly, I used to have the same problem with my little brother. Another thing is that people are always talking in the living room so that even if you can choose the programme, you can't hear it properly.

Rachel: That's a point, although actually I really like talking about what I'm watching, so I don't mind people being around, as long as I can choose the programmes.

Tony: But, why won't your Mum let you have a TV in your room?

Rachel: She says it would cost too much but I don't think that's the real reason, because she said I could have a bike instead. Anyway my Auntie said we could have her old one for next to nothing and my Mum still said no.

Tony: When I got mine my parents were worried that I might watch it late at night and so be too tired for school in the morning. So, I promised them I'd always turn it off before ten o'clock.

Rachel: And do you?

Tony: Not always. It depends what's on.

Rachel: I think my Mum just wants to control what I do, you know, she just wants to be able to say 'No television until you've done your homework', and things like that.

Tony: Perhaps she thinks you need that.

Rachel: She thinks I'm still a child. I'd like the chance to decide things like that for myself.

Tony: My parents never ask about my schoolwork. They say it's something I have to do by myself.

Rachel: You're lucky.

Tony: I know.

Now listen again.

That is the end of Part Four.

You now have six minutes to check and copy your answers on to the answer sheet.

You have one more minute.

That is the end of the test.

TEST 4

PAPER 1 ● Reading and Writing

Reading

Part 1 – Extra material

1a all drivers   1b lorries   1c drive more slowly
2a a camera   2b no   2c Ian and her (can share the cost).
3a no   3b no   3c late because of engineering works
4a visited a castle and went to the beach
4b went sightseeing in the city and looked round the museum   4c looked round the museum
5a no   5b no   5c yes

Exam material

1 C   2 A   3 C   4 B   5 C

Part 2 – Extra material

Question 7: they want to learn other water sports.
Question 8: no information about historic buildings
Question 9: no information about walking in the countryside or climbing
Question 10: no organised activities for the children, no information about walking

Part 2 – Exam material

6 F   7 D   8 G   9 E   10 B

Part 3 – Exam material

11 B   12 A   13 A   14 A   15 B   16 A   17 A
18 A   19 B   20 B

Part 4 – Extra material

1 Michael Sharp
2 People who swim in very cold water
3 Peter Smith and all the swimmers.
4 They all feel fitter.
5 No, he only stayed in 30 seconds.

Part 4 – Exam material

21 A   22 B   23 C   24 A   25 D

Part 5 – Exam material

26 C   27 A   28 D   29 B   30 D   31 A   32 C
33 B   34 C   35 A

Writing

Part 1 – Extra material and Exam material

1 like to / care to
2 for
3 as / so good
4 are 6 / six (people / members / players / musicians)
5 need / have to

Part 2 – Extra material

1 Dan, you + your friends
2 tonight
3 to tell him which cinema you are going to, which film you plan to see and what time you will meet him

Note 1: the film is not named, only described
Note 2: all three points included, but the meeting time is on Saturday, instead of tonight.

Part 2 – Exam material

Question 6: email to Dan

Task-specific Mark Scheme

* information about **which cinema**
* reference to a particular **film**
* mention of **meeting time**

Examiner's comments

See Monika's answer on page 91.

Two content elements are well covered, but the film is described instead of named. This element is therefore only partially communicated.

Band: 4

Examiner's comments

See Boro's answer on page 91.

This is another example where full attention has not been paid to the question, as the meeting is arranged for *Saturday*, instead of *tonight*. Otherwise the three content elements are communicated.

Band: 3

Part 3 – Extra material

Here is a corrected example of the letter on page 92.

> *Dear Sandra,*
>
> *I received your letter last Monday. I hope you are well.*
>
> *I think it is best for you to visit a city because in a city there are lots of interesting places, such as museums, lakes, shops, markets and churches. I think you will like it! In the evening you can go out to eat in a good restaurant and go dancing.*
>
> *In the last week of your holiday you could visit the countryside for two days. It's very quiet and there is some beautiful scenery. You can go walking in the mountains.*
>
> *See you soon.*
>
> *Love,*
> *Natasha*

Part 3 – Exam material

Test 4, Question 7: letter to a friend

Examiner's comments

See the answer on page 92.

This is an inadequate attempt. Although there is some range of language, the numerous errors sometimes impede the meaning and the erratic punctuation leads to incoherence, for example *I think it very better the last week Holiday, we going to visiting …* Considerable effort is required from the reader.

Band: 2

Sample Answer A

> Dear Brian and Dear Suzy,
>
> I was very happy reading in your last lette that you'll visit my country for your next holiday.
>
> I think the best is to spend your time in the city of Geneva. There are lot of things to do, like go sightseeing or shopping. I think you'll enjoy the fountain which is on the Leman Lake.
>
> Obviously, if you'll come to Geneva, you could stay in my flat. It's enough big and I'll really enjoy to see.
>
> I'm waiting for your answer.
>
> I hope I'll see you soo.
>
> Cristina

Examiner's comments

The script shows some evidence of ambition with an adequate range of language and some linking, for example, *Obviously*, and *I think you'll enjoy the fountain which is …* However it is flawed by the number of non-impeding errors, for example *It's enough big* and *I'll really enjoy to see*, which mean that some effort is required from the reader.

Band: 3

Test 4, Question 8: I was really surprised when I read the email

Sample Answer B

> I was really surprised when I read the e-mail: Tom was inviting me to see the new version of Romeo and Julia? I didn't even really know him! After all, where did he get my e-mail adress from? I really didn't know what to do? But then I got a really good idea. I phoned Tom and told him that I would be happy to come, but only if my friend Jasmin can come with us. At first he didn't say anything, then he sighed deeply and agreed.
>
> The next day the three of us went to the cinema. He was really kind and nice. I wouldn't have expected that all! Maybe I should write him an e-mail if he wants to see Bridget Jone's Diary with me …
>
> To be continued …

Examiner's comments

This is a confident and ambitious attempt, for example *After all, where did he get my e-mail adress from?* It is a well organised narrative with a wide range of structures and vocabulary, for example *Tom was inviting me to see the new version …* The errors are minor and non-impeding, for example, *but only if my friend Jasmin can come with us.*

Band: 5

Sample Answer C

> I was surprise when I read the e-mail. It was from my best freind. He said that I hate Mohsen! And I don't want speak him he is not my frein. And he said he is bosy he is dirty I just hate him. Then I got in my car and rush to his hous and I rang the door bel. H was in the house wit my other freind but they didn't want open the door. I was heading back to my car when some body open the door. When I went in some body hit me with a pan!

Examiner's comments

Although the script shows some ambition and attempts at range, for example *I was heading back to my car when some body open the door*, it is let down by numerous errors in tenses, spelling and punctuation, for example *And he said he is bosy he is dirty I just hate him.* This is an inadequate attempt which requires considerable effort from the reader.

Band: 2

Part 1 – Extra material (possible answers)

2 a book, money, box of paints
3 walking by sea; walking in wood; on ship; shorts, dress, trousers
4 apple, money, cola, coloured pencils
5 maths, geography, science
6 4.30, 4.45, 5.15
7 celery, pepper, cauliflower, carrots

Part 1 – Exam material

1 C 2 A 3 B 4 C 5 A 6 B 7 A

Part 2 – Extra material

Question 8: dance music.
Question 9: all like playing this sort of music.
Question 10: you tell them before the party.
Question 11: 12
Question 12: Because he can sing
Question 13: on a cruise boat

Part 2 – Exam material

8 A 9 C 10 A 11 C 12 B 13 B

Part 3 – Exam material

14 1952 / nineteen fifty(-)two
15 S / september
16 (walking / climbing) boots
17 (a route on a) M / map
18 tent
19 (play / playing) table(-)tennis

Part 4 – Exam material

20 A 21 A 22 B 23 B 24 A 25 B

Transcript

This is the Cambridge Preliminary English Test, Test 4.

There are four parts to the test. You will hear each part twice. For each part of the test there will be time for you to look through the questions and time for you to check your answers.

Write your answers on the **question paper**. You will have six minutes at the end of the test to **copy your answers onto the answer sheet**.

The recording will now be stopped.

Please ask any questions now, because you must not speak during the test.

PART 1

Now open your question paper and look at Part One.

There are seven questions in this part. For each question there are three pictures and a short recording.

Choose the correct picture and put a tick in the box below it.

Before we start, here is an example.

How did the woman get to work?

Woman: Oh, I'm so sorry I'm late – I missed the bus. I was trying to decide whether to walk or go back and get my bike when I saw my neighbour. Luckily he offered me a lift, because he works near here.

The first picture is correct so there is a tick in box A.

Look at the three pictures for question 1 now.

Now we are ready to start. Listen carefully. You will hear each recording twice.

One.

Which present has the girl bought her mother?

Jane: Hi … it's me, Jane … I've got Mum's birthday present. I think she'll like it … Yes, that's right, a silver one. She's always writing letters, so she'll find it useful … Mmm. I thought about earrings but she seems to have such a lot of jewellery, and Dad bought her a watch last year. I'm sure she'll like what I've bought.

Now listen again.

Two.

What will the prize be in the painting competition?

Woman: We need to get a prize for the children's painting competition. Last year, Jane won and I think she was given a box of new paints.
Man: It should be something different this time. How about some money? That's always popular.
Woman: Yes, but it would be nice to get them something that reminds them of the competition. I think a book about painting would be a good prize.
Man: You're right. Let's do that.

Now listen again.

Three.

Which photo does the girl dislike?

Girl: I got the photos back! Look, this one of us on the beach is just brilliant!

Boy: Yes … You must get a copy for me to keep as a souvenir. It was a great day, but that other one's good too!

Girl: I don't know why you think so, the dress I'm wearing is awful. I only bought it because it was half-price. The one of us on the boat isn't bad, look.

Boy: Mmm … apart from the fact that you look seasick!

Now listen again.

Four.

What should the students take on the school trip?

Woman: Now you won't need any money for the bus or your entrance ticket to the zoo tomorrow, because that's already paid for. But bring some small change for when you get thirsty and want a drink. The only food or drink allowed on the bus is fruit. Bring some with you because it's a long trip, and you'll get hungry. No food or drink must be taken into the zoo. And you'll need to bring all your coloured pencils for the work I'm going to ask you to do there.

Now listen again.

Five.

Which subject does the boy like best?

Boy: I really like the new chemistry teacher – he let me spend the lesson drawing the equipment for an experiment. The Maths teacher is much more serious, but that's still my favourite subject. I used to like Geography, but the teacher we have now gives us so much homework.

Now listen again.

Six.

What time is the dance class today?

Girl 1: Hi Judy – do you want to play tennis after school – say about 4.15?

Girl 2: Mmm – that would be fun but I've got a dance class. It's usually at a quarter past five but it's half an hour earlier this evening, at a quarter to five. It takes me ages to get into my dance clothes so I really don't think I'll have time today – let's try tomorrow.

Girl 1: OK!

Now listen again.

Seven.

Which vegetables do they decide to put in the curry?

Man: So for the curry, which vegetables do we need to add?

Woman: Well, this celery that I've just washed, although we won't need all of it … and then we'll need some slices of carrot and a yellow pepper if you've got any.

Man: There's one in the bottom of the fridge, but the carrots are a bit old. Could we use this cauliflower instead?

Woman: I don't see why not. Good idea.

Now listen again.

That is the end of Part One.

Now turn to Part Two, questions 8 to 13.

PART 2

You will hear a man talking to a group of people about the band he plays in.

For each question, put a tick in the correct box.

You now have 45 seconds to look at the questions for Part Two.

Now we are ready to start. Listen carefully. You will hear the recording twice.

Bob: My name's Bob, and I've come to tell you about the York Dance Band. Now, if you want to have a good family party, like a wedding or an important birthday, and you want all your guests to dance after dinner, then don't book a noisy disco. Have a live band instead. We play all kinds of dance music, including songs that every age group, from teenagers to grandmothers, can dance to.

The band is made up of all sorts of different people – none of us full-time musicians. We have a doctor, two English teachers, a retired journalist and the band leader owns a hotel. Although none of us has any musical training at all, what we all share is a love of playing this sort of music as a hobby.

That's why, for your party, tell us the type of music you like best; and that's what we'll play. We mostly play songs from the 1970s, but we know lots of more modern songs, and some older ones too! If you have a request for a special song, tell us about a week before the actual day, and we'll make sure we find the music and bring it with us.

The band has been together for ten years, but I only joined six years ago, when they decided to increase the number of members from eight to twelve. I was looking for a band to join, and a friend of mine saw an advertisement in the local paper and persuaded me to apply.

Before I joined, the band didn't have a separate singer, but they realised they needed one. They chose me because I've always enjoyed getting up and singing in front of an audience, and people say I've got a good voice. I've been in bands before, I even played guitar rather badly in one, but this band is easily the best. I even enjoy the practices.

We sometimes meet to practise in a room behind a hotel. It's nice because often when we finish practising a piece, we hear the guests in the nearby hotel restaurant clapping. Occasionally we play at weddings and other parties, but we also perform every Friday evening on a cruise boat that takes tourists up and down the river in York. Everyone has a very good time. We've also just recorded a CD of our favourite songs ... in fact I'll just play a little ...

Now listen again.

That is the end of Part Two.

Now turn to Part Three, questions 14 to 19.

PART 3

You will hear part of a radio programme about climbing holidays in North Wales.

For each question, fill in the missing information in the numbered space.

You now have 20 seconds to look at Part Three.

Now we are ready to start. Listen carefully. You will hear the recording twice.

Man: Today, I want to tell you about the Climbing Centre in the heart of North Wales.

It's a good place to go, whether you're a beginner or more advanced. The Centre was started in 1952 by Peter Evans, the mountaineer, and the building, which used to be a hotel and is very comfortable, dates from 1869. The Climbing Centre shares the site with a management training college. This is open from March to November, but the Climbing Centre itself only runs courses from March until September, although accommodation for climbers is available in the winter months. The Climbing Centre has thirty twin-bedded rooms and ten single rooms providing accommodation for up to 70 people.

I tried a four-day course which I believe was good value at £280. The price includes all food and accommodation, equipment and instruction. However, you do need to take your own walking boots. Make sure they fit you properly and are comfortable.

We spent most of our time on the mountainside learning different things. On the first day we learnt how to plan a route on a map and went out to practise our skills. The next day we learnt how to predict the weather – by looking at the clouds while we were walking. On the third day, we set off for two days' climbing. We had to sleep in a tent so we needed to carry all our food and camping equipment with us.

There aren't many things to do in the evenings at the Centre, apart from watching TV or playing table-tennis. There are cinemas and restaurants in the nearest town, but it's too far to go. People are usually too tired anyway after all the hard work and fresh air they've had during the day.

Now listen again.

That is the end of Part Three.

Now turn to Part Four, questions 20 to 25.

PART 4

Look at the six sentences for this part. You will hear a conversation between a boy, Jack, and a girl, Sarah, about learning to drive.

Decide if each sentence is correct or incorrect. If it is correct, put a tick in the box under A for YES. If it is not correct, put a tick in the box under B for NO.

You now have 20 seconds to look at the questions for Part Four.

Now we are ready to start. Listen carefully. You will hear the recording twice.

Sarah: Hello, Jack. How are the driving lessons going?

Jack: Hi, Sarah. They're fine, but I'm not sure if I like the teacher much. He's not very friendly, really. But I don't suppose that matters too much. He is good at explaining things and I always understand what he wants me to do.

Sarah: That's the important thing.

Jack: But last lesson I had to practise stopping the car quickly – in an emergency – and we also spent some time parking. I've still got a lot to learn. Parking was easy, but I couldn't manage to stop the car quickly enough.

Sarah: It is quite hard the first few times because you have to think very fast.

Jack: Well, I've got three more lessons before my test, and I'm sure I'll be fine on the day.

Sarah: You're feeling confident then?

Jack: Well, it doesn't help to get worried about it, does it?

Sarah: Not really. But three lessons aren't that many. You've only been learning for a couple of months, haven't you?

Jack: Yes. But the lessons are really expensive.

Sarah: I know, but if you don't get enough practice before the test, you might fail. It could be more difficult than you think. Can't your parents take you out to practise?

Jack: They won't do it any more. We went out a few times but they're worried about their car.

Sarah: You could use mine. It's quite old and I don't worry about other people driving it. I passed my test a long time ago, so I can go with you to help you improve.

Jack: Are you sure?

Sarah: Yes. It's fine. Is Sunday all right? I can pick you up about four.

Jack: OK then. Thanks. I'm hoping to get my own car soon. I could never save enough to pay for one myself, but my parents have promised to buy me one if I pass my test. But I need to pass first, and a bit more help would be really good.

Sarah: See you on Sunday then.

Now listen again.

That is the end of Part Four.

You now have six minutes to check and copy your answers on to the answer sheet.

You have one more minute.

That is the end of the test.

Sample answer sheets

UNIVERSITY *of* **CAMBRIDGE**
ESOL Examinations

S A M P L E

Candidate Name
If not already printed, write name
in CAPITALS and complete the
Candidate No. grid (in pencil).

Candidate Signature

Examination Title

Centre

Supervisor:
If the candidate is ABSENT or has WITHDRAWN shade here

Centre No.

Candidate No.

Examination Details

0	0	0	0
1	1	1	1
2	2	2	2
3	3	3	3
4	4	4	4
5	5	5	5
6	6	6	6
7	7	7	7
8	8	8	8
9	9	9	9

PET Paper 1 Reading and Writing Candidate Answer Sheet 1

Instructions

Use a PENCIL (B or HB).

Rub out any answer you want to change with an eraser.

For **Reading:**
Mark ONE letter for each question.
For example, if you think **A** is the right answer to the
question, mark your answer sheet like this:

Part 1	Part 2	Part 3	Part 4	Part 5
1 A B C	6 A B C D E F G H	11 A B	21 A B C D	26 A B C D
2 A B C	7 A B C D E F G H	12 A B	22 A B C D	27 A B C D
3 A B C	8 A B C D E F G H	13 A B	23 A B C D	28 A B C D
4 A B C	9 A B C D E F G H	14 A B	24 A B C D	29 A B C D
5 A B C	10 A B C D E F G H	15 A B	25 A B C D	30 A B C D
		16 A B		31 A B C D
		17 A B		32 A B C D
		18 A B		33 A B C D
		19 A B		34 A B C D
		20 A B		35 A B C D

Continue on the other side of this sheet ➡

S A M P L E

For **Writing (Parts 1 and 2):**

Write your answers clearly in the spaces provided.

Part 1: Write your answers below.	Do not write here
1	1 1 0
2	1 2 0
3	1 3 0
4	1 4 0
5	1 5 0

Part 2 (Question 6): Write your answer below.

Put your answer to Writing Part 3 on Answer Sheet 2 ⟶

UNIVERSITY *of* **CAMBRIDGE**
ESOL Examinations

S A M P L E

Candidate Name
If not already printed, write name
in CAPITALS and complete the
Candidate No. grid (in pencil).

Candidate Signature

Examination Title

Centre

Supervisor:

If the candidate is ABSENT or has WITHDRAWN shade here ⊐

Centre No.

Candidate No.

Examination
Details

0	0	0	0
1	1	1	1
2	2	2	2
3	3	3	3
4	4	4	4
5	5	5	5
6	6	6	6
7	7	7	7
8	8	8	8
9	9	9	9

PET Paper 1 Reading and Writing   Candidate Answer Sheet 2

Candidate Instructions:

Write your answer to Writing Part 3
on the other side of this sheet.

→

Use a PENCIL (B or HB).

This section for use by FIRST Examiner only

Mark:

| 0 | 1.1 | 1.2 | 1.3 | 2.1 | 2.2 | 2.3 | 3.1 | 3.2 | 3.3 | 4.1 | 4.2 | 4.3 | 5.1 | 5.2 | 5.3 |

Examiner Number:

	0 1 2 3 4 5 6 7 8 9
	0 1 2 3 4 5 6 7 8 9
	0 1 2 3 4 5 6 7 8 9
	0 1 2 3 4 5 6 7 8 9

SAMPLE

Part 3: Mark the number of the question you are answering here ➡ Q7 or Q8

Write your answer below.

Do not write below this line

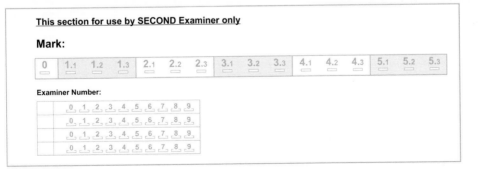

UNIVERSITY *of* **CAMBRIDGE**
ESOL Examinations

S A M P L E

Candidate Name
If not already printed, write name
in CAPITALS and complete the
Candidate No. grid (in pencil).

Candidate Signature

Examination Title

Centre

Supervisor:
If the candidate is ABSENT or has WITHDRAWN shade here ▭

Centre No.

Candidate No.

Examination Details

0	0	0	0
1	1	1	1
2	2	2	2
3	3	3	3
4	4	4	4
5	5	5	5
6	6	6	6
7	7	7	7
8	8	8	8
9	9	9	9

PET Paper 2 Listening Candidate Answer Sheet

You must transfer all your answers from the Listening Question Paper to this answer sheet.

Instructions

Use a PENCIL (B or HB).

Rub out any answer you want to change with an eraser.

For **Parts 1, 2** and **4:**
Mark ONE letter for each question.
For example, if you think **A** is the right answer to the question, mark your answer sheet like this:

`0` A ▬ C

For **Part 3:**
Write your answers clearly in the spaces next to the numbers (14 to 19) like this:

`0` example

Part 1	Part 2	Part 3	Do not write here	Part 4
1 A B C	8 A B C	14	1 14 0	20 A B
2 A B C	9 A B C	15	1 15 0	21 A B
3 A B C	10 A B C	16	1 16 0	22 A B
4 A B C	11 A B C	17	1 17 0	23 A B
5 A B C	12 A B C	18	1 18 0	24 A B
6 A B C	13 A B C	19	1 19 0	25 A B
7 A B C				

Cambridge Exams Extra – PET CD-ROM

This CD-ROM provides an introduction to the computer-based PET. It contains the same four Reading and Writing papers and the same four Listening papers that appear in the book. The questions on the CD-ROM are exactly the same as the questions in the book, but the CD-ROM enables you to try these questions on screen in the same format as they appear in the computer-based PET. All of the questions on the CD-ROM are fully interactive, and are designed to allow you to practise at your own pace before attempting a test under exam conditions.

CD-ROM instructions for PC

1 Insert the CD into your CD-ROM drive.
2 Follow the installation instructions that appear on screen.
3 If installation does not begin automatically, open 'My Computer', then browse to your CD-ROM drive and double click on the 'Setup' icon.

CD-ROM instructions for Mac OSX

1 Insert the CD into your CD-ROM drive.
2 Open the CD-ROM folder and drag the *PET-Extra* folder to your desktop.
3 Open the *PET-Extra* folder and double click on the *PET* icon.

System requirements

For PC
Essential: Windows 2000 and Windows XP
Recommended: 400 MHz processor or faster, with 128MB of RAM or more

For Mac
Essential: Mac OSX, version 10.3 or higher
Recommended: 400 MHz G3 processor or faster, with 128MB of RAM or more